# The 21 Most Effective Prayers of the Bible

Dave Earley

**BARBOUR**
PUBLISHING

Cover image © Garborg Design Works, Inc., Savage, Minnesota

Published by Barbour Publishing, Inc., P.O. Box 719, Uhrichsville, Ohio 44683
www.barbourbooks.com

*Our mission is to publish and distribute inspirational products offering exceptional value and biblical encouragement to the masses.*

 Member of the
Evangelical Christian
Publishers Association

Printed in the United States of America.
5 4 3 2 1

*c19*

# DEDICATION

This book is dedicated in loving memory of
Bob S. Earley.
The last few years of his life
Dad's prayers grew in frequency, fervency, and impact.
He loved praying the prayers of the Bible, and especially,
"God bless me that I might bless others." And God did.

# ACKNOWLEDGMENTS

No man is an island and no successful book is a solo effort.
Many thanks to the team of people who made this project a
reality:

- Cathy for loving me, believing in me, and allowing me to
  serve God in this way
- My boys, Daniel, Andrew, and Luke, for praying for me
- Carol, my favorite sister and the best PR person I could ever
  imagine
- Susan for all of her help with the details of the church
- The Mighty Men for their prayers
- Paul Muckley, an awesome guy and good friend who went the
  extra mile to make this project effective
- Ellen Caughey for her editorial expertise, Kelly Williams for
  managing the in-house editorial process, and Glady Dunlap
  for handling the typesetting
- Rich Nathan, Rhonda Tucker, Roy Mansfeld, and Andy Bul-
  lard for allowing me to tell their stories
- Bob and Rusty Russell, Bruce Wilkinson, Henry Blackaby,
  and David Jeremiah for helping me learn more about prayer

# Contents

# INTRODUCTION

Don't you just love it when a plan comes together? Isn't it awesome when you try something and it actually works?

I have little ability when it comes to fixing things—and, unfortunately, all five of the people in my household are gifted at breaking things. Being the dad, I am the first one called upon, though I'm not sure why. My efforts often end in failure, or I make things worse than they were. But on rare and glorious occasions, the thing-a-ma-jig gets fixed. That's when the band plays, there's dancing in the streets, and all is right with the world.

Through the years one of the true joys in my prayer life has come from praying the actual prayers of the Bible, especially those that worked. I reason that if God answered the petitions of Hannah, David, and Jacob, He might do the same for me—and He has!

Recently I accepted the challenge to narrow the hundreds of prayers in the Bible to twenty-one short, simple petitions that God answered positively. These twenty-one high-impact prayers span thousands of years, come from all classes of people, and were offered for a variety of reasons. Each was particular and direct, expressed with great earnestness, and offered with sincere expectation. They were offered as requests, not demands. They flow in conformity with the life of the requester and were presented with genuine reverence and humility. And they were all wonderfully answered!

They are petitions God enjoyed enough to have recorded as Scripture. They changed the lives of those who prayed them—and they are requests that we can make today. I have found that praying the answered prayers of the Bible gives me confidence that what I am asking is at least close to the will of God.

> *Learning them is fun.*
> *Remembering them is easy.*
> *Praying them is simple.*
> *Seeing God answer them is exciting.*

Praying these petitions will become an adventure that can change your life. However, before you do, let me remind you of some important truths about prayer. I agree with Bob Russell's warning that prayer is not dictation. Prayer is not telling God what to do and then expecting His immediate, positive response. Prayer is cooperating with God so that He can release His power.[1]

Someone said that God answers prayers, "Yes," "No," "Wait," and "You gotta be kidding." Someone else said that if our request is wrong, God says, "No"; if our timing is wrong, God says, "Slow"; if we are wrong, God says, "Grow"; and if our request is right, our timing is right, and we are right, God says, "Go!" However God answers, we know that He is a wise heavenly Father who knows what is best for us, and what is best for others.

When my youngest son, Luke, was three, he began asking me for a pocketknife. Repeatedly, he received the same answer: "Wait until you are old enough so you won't hurt yourself or your brothers." Yet, he kept asking. When he was five and a half, his mother, taken with a genuine Swiss Army knife in a store window, purchased the knife. The end of the story is that Luke ended up needing three stitches in his leg. (That is one of the few times I said to my wife, *I told you so.*)

Even if you do pray the most effective prayers in the Bible, like my son, you may not always get the answer you want when you want it. God's "No" or "Wait" is another way of saying, "I love you and I only give what is best for you." Keep in mind God is not our servant—but we are His. He answers according to *His* plans and purposes, and not ours. Our heavenly Father knows best.

I think you will find that He delights in saying, "Yes." God loves to hear and answer prayers. More often than not, He is the God of "Yes."

## Features for More Effective Prayer

This book features three aids to enhance your prayer life:

1. *A Prayer to Remember and to Pray.* Each chapter highlights a short, simple, significant prayer. Most are only four or five words in length. Try to memorize each one so you will always have it available when you need it.

2. *A Chapter to Read.* There are twenty-two chapters in this book. Make a goal to read one chapter every day for the next three weeks (plus one day). If that is unrealistic, try for one every other day.

3. *Scriptures to Study.* Each prayer is taken from the life of a Bible character. I suggest that you open your Bible to the passage discussed and mark it. These are some of the most fascinating and often overlooked stories in the Bible. You will want to go back to them later.

## Suggestions for More Effective Prayer

1. *A Time to Pray.* Try to determine a set time each day when you will read a chapter and pray. It could be first thing in the morning or the last thing at night, or over your lunch hour. The right time is the time that works for you.

2. *An Amount of Time for Prayer.* There are 24 hours in a

day, or 1,440 minutes. Setting aside 15, or 30, or 60 minutes a day for study and prayer can become a life-changing experience. Oliver Wendell Holmes said that a mind is like a rubber band—once stretched it never returns to its original size. Pick an amount of time that will stretch you. Even if you can't maintain that schedule after the three weeks is over, you will have experienced significant growth in your prayer life.

3. *A Place for Prayer.* Jesus spoke of a prayer closet. Your place for prayer could be at a desk or the kitchen table or on your bed. I often enjoy taking a prayer walk in the middle of the day. The right place is the place that is right for you.

4. *A Friend with Whom to Pray.* Jesus promised added insight and answers when two or more agree in prayer (Matthew 18:19). Ask a friend to read this book along with you. Gather together face to face, or over the phone, and pray together the prayers you are learning.

As a final note, the twenty-one prayers that follow have been ordered as they appear in the Bible. Although there are many ways the prayers could have been presented, I hope God will bless you as you discover the growing spiritual maturity evidenced in this biblical progression.

## NOTES

[1]Bob Russell and Rusty Russell, *When God Answers Prayer* (West Monroe, LA: Howard Publishing Company, 2003), pp. 10–14.

# 1

# GIVE ME SUCCESS TODAY:

*The Prayer of Eliezer*

GENESIS 24:12

Are you due for some success? If so, the prayer of Eliezer is a good place to start.

The story begins with Abraham, a recent widower, arriving at the ripe old age of 140 years. Abraham seriously wanted his son, Isaac, to marry and give him a grandson. Isaac was already forty years old and hopelessly single. So Abraham took action.

Abraham called his chief servant, Eliezer, and sent him on an ancient version of Mission Impossible. He would have to travel 450 rigorous miles by camel to the area where Abraham grew up. There he was to select a suitable bride for Isaac. She would have to be from among Abraham's distant relatives (the custom was to marry a first cousin). After finding such a girl, he would then have to convince her to return with him to marry Isaac, a man she had never met. This would be no walk in the park.

Eliezer gathered a small caravan and made the lengthy trek to Abraham's homeland. His plan was to find the right girl at the central meeting place for desert communities—the well. As he approached the town, he offered a simple prayer:

*"O LORD, God of my master Abraham, give me success today, and show kindness to my master Abraham. See, I am standing beside this spring, and the daughters of the townspeople are coming out to draw water. May it be that when I say to a girl, 'Please let down your jar that I may have a drink,' and she says, 'Drink, and I'll water your camels too'—let her be the one you have chosen for your servant Isaac. By this I will know that you have shown kindness to my master."*

GENESIS 24:12–14

### Give me success today.

Notice the core of his prayer: "Give me success today." This request was simple, specific, and definite in reference to time. He asked God to direct him to the right girl and do it right away. After all, Isaac was not getting any younger. In order to know which girl would be the right one, Eliezer added to his request that she not merely offer to get him a drink but also volunteer to water his camels.

"Give me success today" was a wee, little prayer. Yet it immediately reaped a stupendous, prodigious answer! Look at the glorious results:

*Before he had finished praying, Rebekah came out with her jar on her shoulder. She was the daughter of Bethuel son of Milcah, who was the wife of Abraham's brother Nahor. The girl was very beautiful, a virgin; no man had ever lain with her. She went down to the spring, filled her jar and came up again. The servant hurried to meet her and said, "Please give me a little water from your jar." "Drink, my lord," she said, and quickly lowered the jar*

*to her hands and gave him a drink. After she had given*
*him a drink, she said, "I'll draw water for your camels*
*too, until they have finished drinking."*

GENESIS 24:15–19

Bingo! God hit the target. He answered Eliezer's prayer and then some. *Before he had finished praying,* God sent the right girl. Rebekah, as it turned out, was a distant relative of Abraham, which meant she was qualified. Not insignificantly, she also happened to be a very beautiful and unattached virgin. To top it off, she not only gave Eliezer a drink, but she also offered to water his camels!

And that's not all. Later we read that Rebekah was willing to leave her family and her home immediately to make the return trip with Eliezer (24:58). The story even has a happy ending—when Isaac met her, he loved her (24:67).

God did not merely answer Eliezer's request with a timid, little "Yes." His answer was a robust, overwhelming "YES!" Yes, a girl offered to give Eliezer water. Yes, she asked to water his camels as well. Yes, she was related to Abraham. Yes, she was beautiful. Yes, she was an available virgin. Yes, she was willing to travel with him all the way back to marry Isaac. And for the two of them, yes, it was love at first sight.

Furthermore, God's "Yes" blessed everyone involved. Abraham had the good fortune of gaining a non-Canaanite daughter-in-law to be the mother of his grandson. Rebekah became an essential part of God's promise to Abraham that he would become the father of many nations. For Rebekah, she received a husband who loved her and a place in the royal line of the Messiah. She moved from a pagan family to a God-fearing one. Isaac's life was changed because he received a very beautiful bride. Rebekah would be the woman he would love and who would bear his sons.

But the greatest windfall came to Eliezer. Prior to this event, Eliezer viewed God solely as Abraham's God. Instead of a personal relationship with the Lord, he had more of a secondhand relationship. But after he experienced the loving and powerful way God answered his prayer, he became a man who worshiped God for himself (Genesis 24:26–27).

Eliezer now had his own story to tell. He eagerly told Rebekah's older brother all that the Lord had done for him (see Genesis 24:34–48). Because of this answered prayer, he had his own testimony to share of how God had worked on his behalf.

Now the way I figure it, if God would do that for Eliezer when he prayed, "Give me success," He might be willing to do the same for me, and for you.

### Making It Personal

One tiny prayer had a tremendous impact on many lives. As we read the story of this ancient prayer, we find several lessons for our lives today.

1. *Prayer is for everyone.* Although we assume the servant was Eliezer, we do not know for sure. Chapter 24 simply calls him "the chief servant of Abraham."[1] But nothing in the Word of God is written the way it is by accident. Eliezer may be intentionally unnamed to remind us that answered prayer is not the privileged domain of the big-name, spiritual elite. It is the heritage of all who call upon the Lord.

2. *God answered a selfish-sounding prayer.* Eliezer prayed, "Give *me* success today"—and God answered in the affirmative. While we may have been convinced it is wrong to pray

selfish-sounding prayers, as a result, we are missing many of the blessings God intended.

In the biblical record, God answered some selfish-sounding prayers when they were offered with legitimate motives and for beneficial things. Eliezer's request, while appearing selfish, was also *selfless*, in that he wanted God to answer in order to ultimately serve his master. He was not praying about his own bride but a bride for another man, Isaac. And, if the unnamed servant is indeed Eliezer, then this request was especially unselfish, as Eliezer was sent to get a bride for the man who took his place as Abraham's heir (Genesis 15:2)!

3. *God is very eager to answer prayer.* Notice those first four words in Genesis 24:15: "Before he finished praying." God was already answering *before* Eliezer was finished praying! Rebekah came out with her jar on her shoulder *before* Eliezer had even completed his petition. When we ask for good things with worthy motives, God may respond quickly.

Often we have the misconception that God is reluctant to answer prayer. We think that He must be begged or manipulated or argued into answering. I have come to assume that when it comes to asking in prayer, I have nothing to lose. If mine is not the right request offered at the right time, or if my motives are not quite right, what is the worst that can happen? God can say "No."

But if my request is something to which God can say "Yes," then by asking I may receive a blessing I would not have obtained otherwise. I would rather go to my grave being guilty of asking for more than I received than for missing answers because I did not ask.

4. *When you pray for success, give God a specific target.* Eliezer asked that a very special girl would not only be willing to give

him a drink, but that she would also offer to water his camels (24:14). Too often we get vague blessings because we pray vague prayers. If we want specific answers, we need to make specific requests.

I learned the power of specific prayer as a sophomore at a rather strict college. I needed a haircut or I would be in violation of the school hair code. One evening my resident assistant gave me twenty-four hours to get a haircut. I had absolutely no money and no hope of getting a decent haircut for free. (My three roommates had proven to be notorious "butchers" who no sane person would trust with a pair of scissors.)

Later that night I was reading in Luke 11 where Jesus told the story of the persistent friend. The passage encourages specific prayer as the man asks for *three* loaves. So I gave God a specific threefold target: I asked Him for (1) a good haircut, (2) before the next evening ended, and (3) for free. As I prayed, I received a wonderful sense of peace. Soon I dozed off to sleep.

The next day I overslept and ran out to class, forgetting all about my need for a haircut. But God didn't forget. That evening at the dinner table a friend introduced me to a girl I had never met. As we talked, she said that she had graduated from beauty school and her dad had made her attend a liberal arts college for a semester. She said that she really missed cutting hair and was thinking of starting her own business on the side. Then she looked at me and said, "You have a nice head of hair. Hmm, I miss cutting hair so much, I would cut yours for free."

After dinner I could not help but smile as I sat in a chair listening to her whistle and watching the hair drop around my feet. God had heard my simple, specific prayer. He had given me a great haircut, in less than twenty-four hours, for free.

I asked for success and God answered. I had a need and God

met it. When given a target to hit, God drilled a bull's-eye.[2]

Need an answer? Can you use some success in a God-directed assignment? Why not give God a target to hit? He might just answer, "Yes!" He might even say, "YES!"

## NOTES

[1] The servant's name is not stated in Genesis 24:2. He is simply referred to as "the chief servant of Abraham." Scholars assume that this servant was Eliezer, whom Abraham trusted enough to consider making his heir (Genesis 15). For a more detailed discussion, see note for Genesis 24:2 in John MacArthur, *The MacArthur Study Bible* (Nashville, TN: Word Publishing, 1997), p. 46.

[2] For more on prayer for success, see Dave Earley, *Prayer Odyssey* (Shippensburg, PA: Destiny Image Publishers, 2003), pp. 37–40.

# 2

## BLESS ME:

### *The Prayer of Jacob*

#### GENESIS 32:26

As they say where I grew up, Jacob was "in a fix." Years before, he had taken the birthright blessing meant for his older brother, Esau, and Esau had not forgotten. Keep in mind that Esau was a burly, roughhewn, angry man. Not the sort you would want to meet in a dark alley.

Now Esau was bearing down on Jacob with an army of four hundred men. The best plan Jacob could devise was to use Middle Eastern strategy and send Esau a series of carefully selected gifts, even though he had little hope that this would work.

At that point Jacob did what desperate men should do. He prayed (Genesis 32:9–12), but he didn't sound very sincere, apparently even to himself. Thus, he continued to try and wiggle out of sure disaster (Genesis 32:13–24), and ended up finding himself alone and even more desperate (Genesis 32:24).

A man appeared in the dark to Jacob and a battle began. Arms were twisted, legs were seized, and necks were wrenched. All through the night the wrestling war was waged. When it became clear Jacob could not win, he grabbed hold of the stranger and hung on for dear life. Then he uttered a small prayer: "I will not let you go unless you bless me" (Genesis 32:26).

**Bless me.**

Jacob had taken hold of God—his opponent in the dark—and refused to let go until God had blessed him. Asking for all the blessing he could get was typical of Jacob. He had asked his father to give him the biggest blessing his father could give and now he was asking the same of God.

When I first read this story I was surprised at the boldness, the brashness, and yes, the greediness of Jacob. Come on! I was expecting God to rise up and blast him for making such a request. Instead, God gave Jacob what he asked for. God blessed him with a manifold blessing—one replete with transformation, revelation, direction, protection, and impact.

> *The man asked him, "What is your name?" "Jacob," he answered. Then the man said, "Your name will no longer be Jacob, but Israel, because you have struggled with God and with men and have overcome."*
>
> GENESIS 32:27–28

God changed his name from Jacob, meaning "grasper," to Israel, meaning "prince of God." The name change indicated a transformation of heart. There is a positive side to Jacob's personality, and God was obviously impressed with his prevailing perseverance. He had held on, and hung on, until he got what he sought. When he had a chance to get a hold of God, he refused to let go.

> *Jacob said, "Please tell me your name." But he replied, "Why do you ask my name?" Then he blessed him there. So Jacob called the place Peniel, saying, "It is because I saw God face to face, and yet my life was spared." The sun rose*

*above him as he passed Peniel, and he was limping because
of his hip. Therefore to this day the Israelites do not eat the
tendon attached to the socket of the hip, because the socket
of Jacob's hip was touched near the tendon.*

GENESIS 32:29–32

When Jacob chose the Hebrew word *Peniel,* which means
"the face of God," to commemorate the site, he was clearly
aware that he had been given a rare and glorious opportunity.
He had a face-to-face encounter with the living God and lived
to tell about it. At Peniel, God revealed Himself to Jacob in a
life-changing way. God touched his hip and changed the way
he walked the rest of his life. More importantly, God touched
his heart and changed the way he lived the rest of his life.

*Jacob looked up and there was Esau, coming with his
four hundred men; so he divided the children among
Leah, Rachel and the two maidservants. He put the
maidservants and their children in front, Leah and her
children next, and Rachel and Joseph in the rear. He
himself went on ahead and bowed down to the ground
seven times as he approached his brother.*

GENESIS 33:1–3

God gave Jacob a plan, one that would require something
new for Jacob. He would take the path of humility. When Jacob
went and faced his brother, he bowed low before him seven times
as an inferior would before a highly honored patron.

*But Esau ran to meet Jacob and embraced him; he threw
his arms around his neck and kissed him. And they wept.*

GENESIS 33:4

Instead of killing Jacob, Esau embraced him and kissed him. Together they wept. Years of deep bitterness and guilt were erased in a few moments. God had blessed Jacob with protection in the face of sure death.

This little prayer caused lives to be changed! All those with Jacob—his wives, children, servants, and livestock—were spared. Among those was his son, Judah, from whom the Messiah would descend. So, in a sense, Jacob's prayer blessed all of us.

Beyond that, Esau's life was wonderfully altered. He let go of a lifetime of bitterness toward his overly aggressive brother. Instead of killing Jacob, he embraced him.

Yet, the biggest change was seen in the life of Jacob. Jacob not only had a new name, but he had a new heart. Notice how this story ends.

> [Esau asked,] "What do you mean by all this company I have met?" And he said, "To find favor in the sight of my lord." But Esau said, "I have plenty, my brother; let what you have be your own." Jacob said, "No, please, if I have found favor in your sight, then take my present from my hand, for I see your face as one sees the face of God, and you have received me favorably. Please take my gift which has been brought to you, because God has dealt graciously with me and because I have plenty." Thus he urged him and he took it.
>
> GENESIS 33:8–11 NASB

Can you imagine Jacob begging Esau to "please take my blessing"? Jacob, the one who previously had stolen the blessing, was now eager to give a blessing. He was a new man. He humbly acknowledged that God had blessed him. Therefore, he desired to bless others.

## Making It Personal

1. *God blesses the spiritually aggressive.* The blessing of God does not necessarily rest on the passive or the lax. I think that somewhere along the line we have developed the mistaken notion that Christians are nice, quiet, almost wimpy people.

Nothing could be further from the truth. While we are to be gracious and kind, God wants us to be much more than really nice people. He dreams of His people winning battles, relishing adventures, and enjoying all that He has for us.

One man describes it this way: "Prayer is not a lovely sedan for a sightseeing trip around the city. Prayer is a truck that goes straight to the warehouse, backs up, loads, and comes home with the goods. Too many people rattle their trucks all over town and never back up to the warehouse! They do not go after something when they pray. They do not ask, therefore, they do not receive."[1]

I have to admit that I have a quiet, timid streak. My mother was a Quaker and I was raised to cast a skeptical eye on bold, aggressive people. But timidity must not be confused with humility. God blesses humility, not timidity. He also invites boldness in prayer.[2]

A few years ago we decided to have a special Sunday at our church when everyone would bring unchurched friends to the worship services. The week before that Sunday I had made the bold assertion that I believed if we asked God to bless us, we could see fifty adults giving their hearts to Jesus Christ. Afterward, my wife calmly reminded me how I had stuck my neck out.

In preparation for Sunday, hundreds of our members were fasting and praying. Many of us got alone and wrestled with God. I boldly, and maybe a bit desperately, asked Him to bless us with a record attendance and fifty decisions for Christ.

At that time we had three Sunday services. At the conclusion of the first, a handful of people responded to the opportunity to trust Christ as Savior. The second service concluded with a dozen giving their hearts to Jesus. I was very excited for our new brothers and sisters in the faith, but we would need to have thirty-four decisions in the last service to reach fifty.

The third service was packed and everything went well. I gave the invitation to trust Christ and one by one, dozens of people began to respond. After the service ended one of our other pastors grabbed me. "Fifty," he said with a huge grin. "Can you believe it? I counted a total of fifty adults trusting Christ as Savior today!"

Immediately after that, a handful of men walked up to me with curious looks on their faces. They were the prayer team who had spent the entire service in another part of the building getting hold of God and asking Him to bless that day. They had one question they had to ask: "How many?"

I teased them, "How many what?"

"How many people met Jesus as Savior today?" they asked eagerly. "We felt led to ask God to bless us with fifty," they said. "So how many were there?"

I grinned and said, "You should have asked for fifty-one."

2. *God is willing and able to bless those who ask.* God loves to rain down favors on the lives of His children. He wants to benefit us as much as we can stand. It may not be according to our when, where, or how, but God wants to bless His children! According to Bruce Wilkinson, writing in *The Prayer of Jabez*, "The very nature of God is to have goodness in so much abundance that it overflows into our unworthy lives. If you think about God differently than that, I am asking you to change the way you think. Why not make it a lifelong commitment to ask God every day to bless you—while He's at it, bless you *a lot.*"[3]

3. *God's blessing is big enough to go beyond us to others.* Jacob asked God to bless him, but he was not the only one blessed. His family, his brother, and ultimately through Messiah, all of us were blessed.

4. *Receiving God's blessing should make us the "blessers" of others.* Being the recipients of God's generous grace should make us graciously generous. God is all about others. Everything He does in us and for us is designed to eventually flow through us to others.

5. *God reveals Himself to those who really want to know Him.* God Himself is the ultimate blessing. Jacob's greatest blessing was not that his brother spared him, but that he got to see God, touch God, and hear God. It doesn't get any better than that!

Here's one final thought on Jacob's prayer: There are no miracles without messes and no need for blessing if we have it all already. So, if there is a blessing you really need or want and could use to bless others, and you believe that God would want you to have it, then don't be shy. Go ahead and ask. God is able and, as we saw with Jacob, He blesses the spiritually aggressive.

### NOTES

[1] J. R. Rice, *Prayer: Asking and Receiving* (Murfreesboro, TN: Sword of the Lord, 1942), p. 52.

[2] See Hebrews 4:16.

[3] Bruce Wilkinson, *The Prayer of Jabez* (Sisters, OR: Multnomah Publishers, 2000), pp. 28–29.

# GO WITH US:

## *The Prayer of Moses*

EXODUS 33:15

Poor guy. Moses faced one of the most difficult leadership challenges in history. He had to lead a million whining slaves out of Egypt, through the desert wilderness, and into the Promised Land. Every time he turned around, his people were either rebelling or griping.

One of the lowest points came when Moses descended from Mount Sinai carrying the Ten Commandments, only to come upon a riotous party at which the people were worshiping dumb idols. God would have annihilated the Hebrew people had Moses not interceded (Exodus 32:9–14).

How was Moses supposed to guide the people safely through the hazards of the desert into the Promised Land without them destroying him or themselves?

In answer, Moses prayed.

*Now Moses used to take a tent and pitch it outside the camp some distance away, calling it the "tent of meeting."*
*. . .As Moses went into the tent, the pillar of cloud would come down and stay at the entrance, while the Lord spoke with Moses. Whenever the people saw the pillar of cloud standing at the entrance to the tent, they all stood*

*and worshiped, each at the entrance to his tent. The Lord would speak to Moses face to face, as a man speaks with his friend.*

Exodus 33:7–11

Moses was a man of effective prayer. Moses had a *place* where he met with God—the tent of meeting—far away from the hustle of humanity. When Moses went into the tent to meet God, God came into the tent to meet Moses. Moses understood something we must remember: *God is willing, ready, and available to meet with us when we make time to meet with Him.*

Moses had very personal meetings with God. "The Lord spoke with Moses face to face, as a man speaks with his friend." Nothing was hidden. It was a dear and daily dialogue, as well as a close and consistent conversation. Moses had developed, probably on the backside of the desert during his forty years of exile, a familiar friendship with God. That is the secret of inner strength, and that is the foundation of effective prayer.

Out of this friendship Moses voiced his complaint.

*Moses said to the LORD, "You have been telling me, 'Lead these people,' but you have not let me know whom you will send with me."*

Exodus 33:12

Forty years earlier Moses had tried to deliver Israel in his own strength only to fail miserably. Now he knew that he needed God. Without God, the entire endeavor would be a tragic nightmare. Without God it was hopeless.

Moses needed the presence of God. There was no other way. Yet, he not only recognized his need, he acted on it. Moses was ultimately successful because he asked God for help, praying one of the most effective prayers in the Bible.

> *"You have said, 'I know you by name and you have found favor with me.' If you are pleased with me, teach me your ways so I may know you and continue to find favor with you. Remember that this nation is your people." The LORD replied, "My Presence will go with you, and I will give you rest." Then Moses said to him, "If your Presence does not go with us, do not send us up from here."*
>
> EXODUS 33:12–15

## Go with us.

"If your Presence does not go with us, do not send us up from here." In other words, "Your presence is the key to our peace, protection, and prosperity. Go with us. Your presence is the source of our survival and success. Without You there will soon be none of us."

> *"How will anyone know that you are pleased with me and with your people unless you go with us? What else will distinguish me and your people from all the other people on the face of the earth?"*
>
> EXODUS 33:16

Moses prayed, "Go with us." He was saying, "Lord, Your presence is the mark of Your pleasure. Your attendance sets us apart. You are distinctly divine. Without You we are nothing but a tragic troop tramping aimlessly into oblivion."

So Moses asked God to go with them. And God said, "Yes."

*And the LORD said to Moses, "I will do the very thing you have asked, because I am pleased with you and I know you by name."*

EXODUS 33:17

From that moment, God's presence marked Moses' life. In fact, God was so manifestly with him that Moses' face actually glowed.

*When Moses came down from Mount Sinai with the two tablets of the Testimony in his hands, he was not aware that his face was radiant because he had spoken with the LORD.*

EXODUS 34:29

## Making It Personal

Moses isn't the only one with a dire requirement for the presence of God. If you and I ever hope to fulfill God's plan for our lives, we need God. His presence must accompany us. His being must cover us like a cloud and emanate from us like perfume. He must go with us.

A few years ago as I was reading the Bible, I discovered that embedded in the defining moments of the lives of key people in the Bible is the little phrase, "God was with him." God's presence was the determining factor.

The things we want and need most in life come from God. They are only realized when His presence is manifest with us. Read down through this "grocery list" of the staggering blessings and benefits attending God's people when He accompanies them.

Individual protection and provision—Genesis 28:15, 20
Deliverance and transformation—Acts 7:9

Prosperity in the face of grave adversity—Genesis 39:2

Favor with ungodly authorities—Genesis 39:21

Success—Genesis 39:23; 1 Samuel 18:12,14; 1 Chronicles
17:2; 2 Kings 18:7

National protection—Numbers 14:8

Blessings—Numbers 23:21

Destruction of fear—Deuteronomy 31:6, 8; Joshua 1:9;
Psalm 118:6

Godly influence—Joshua 6:27

Courage—Judges 6:12

Victory—Judges 1:19, 22; Isaiah 8:10

Guarantee of God's promises—1 Samuel 3:19

Transformation and power—1 Samuel 10:6–7

Qualification for leadership—1 Samuel 16:18

Greatness—2 Samuel 7:9; 2 Chronicles 1:1; 1 Kings 1:37

Encouragement—1 Chronicles 28:20

Magnetic ability to draw a large following—
2 Chronicles 15:9

Confidence—Psalm 118:7; 2 Chronicles 13:12; Jeremiah
20:11; Zechariah 10:5

Evident favor of God—Luke 1:28

Miraculous power—Acts 10:38

I say, sign me up! No wonder Moses prayed, "Go with us."

Moses is not the only one to ask God for his presence. A study of biographies of noted Christians indicates that many have enjoyed this sweet secret of spiritual success and rest. Indeed, the three men who may have had the greatest impact on western Christianity in the eighteenth and nineteenth centuries had one common characteristic: They were indelibly marked by the presence of God.

John Wesley was the father of the great spiritual awakening that shook England and America as well as the founder of the Methodist church. He is surely one of the most influential Christians who ever lived. One of his many biographers noted, "He was a man who sought to keep the glow of God in his life shining at such a white heat that others should recognize it and be led to seek the same transforming power."[1]

Charles Finney was a lawyer who was dramatically converted to Christianity and immediately began to preach in small towns in upstate New York. They say that when Finney entered a town, the presence of God was so thick people either repented or died. Finney and his associates spent hours fervently begging God for powerful manifestations of His presence.

On one occasion, he had been holding a revival at a little place called New York Mills. One morning he was asked to tour the large cotton mill in town. As he walked into the mill, the presence of God became so thick that God began to convict the people there immediately. He entered a large room where the young women working at the looms were laughing and joking. Soon the room grew still. One of the girls looked into his eyes and began to tremble. Her finger began to shake and she broke her thread. One record stated, "She was quite overcome, and sank down, and burst into tears. The impression caught like powder and in a few moments all of the room was in tears. The feeling spread through the factory."[2]

Another biographer has noted, "The owner heard the equipment stopping, and came in to see what was going on. When he saw that the whole room was in tears, he told the superintendent to stop the mill, for it was more important for souls to be saved than for the mill to run. Up to that point Finney had not said a word. The workers assembled in a large room. And in a few days almost all the employees of the mill were saved."[3]

Charles Finney did not have to say a thing! God's presence was so powerful on his life that a mill full of workers repented without him saying a word.

D. L. Moody started a great church, an outstanding college, and is said to have introduced one million souls to Jesus Christ. Early in his ministry he was a highly dedicated man who tirelessly labored to bring souls one by one to Christ. His dear friend, Ira Sankey, described him at this period of his life as "a great hustler; he had a tremendous desire to do something, but he had no real power. He worked very largely in the energy of the flesh."[4]

During a trip to England, Moody's heart was ignited to somehow reach more people for Christ than he was reaching. Yet, he wasn't up to the task. So he began to wrestle with the Lord in prayer. Years later he shared what happened.

*About four years ago I got into a cold state. It did not seem as if there was any unction [power] resting upon my ministry. For four long months God seemed to be just showing me myself. . . . But after four months the anointing came. It came upon me as I was walking in the streets of New York. Many a time I have thought of it since I have been here. At last I had returned to God again, and I was wretched no longer. I almost prayed in my joy, "O stay Thy hand!" I thought this earthen vessel would break. He filled me so full of the Spirit.*

*If I have not been a different man since, I do not know myself. I think I have accomplished more in the last four years than in all the rest of my life.[5]*

Soon afterward God allowed Moody to make global impact and the results of his efforts were incredibly multiplied. The only explanation was the manifest presence of God.

Consider these examples: Wesley sought God for His presence and it marked his life and ministry; Finney and his associates wrestled with God for the manifestation of His presence; Moody deeply and passionately desired God's presence to go with Him and consume his life; and Moses refused to go a step farther without the manifest presence of God.

If your life and ministry is lacking the spark of God's power, the favor of the Spirit's anointing, or the aura of divine protection, you need a greater manifestation of the presence of God. Learn to pray Moses' prayer, "Go with me."

## NOTES

[1] Basil Miller, *John Wesley* (Minneapolis, MN: Bethany House Publishers, 1969), p. 131.

[2] Idem, *Charles Finney* (Minneapolis, MN: Bethany House Publishers, 1969), p. 55.

[3] Wesley Duewel, *Revival Fires* (Grand Rapids, MI: Zondervan, 1995), p. 103.

[4] R. A. Torrey, *Why God Used D. L. Moody* (Murfreesboro, TN: Sword of the Lord, 2000), p. 29.

[5] Ibid., p. 30.

# Give Me a Sign:

## The Prayer of Gideon

### Judges 6:17

At certain desperate points in life we all wish we had something
—preferably an undeniably clear sign!—to let us know which
direction to take. But have you ever needed to know, beyond
a shadow of a doubt, that the desires of your heart are God's
divine desires for your life?

In Israel around 1200 BC a man named Gideon was mind-
ing his own business when God appeared and called him to
deliver his nation from an oppressive enemy. How did he know
it was God? How was he sure he was hearing God's instructions
clearly? Gideon needed answers. He needed a sign.

As happened repeatedly, Israel had wandered from following
God, and so God had removed His hand of protection. Con-
sequently, camel raiders freely swooped in on the Israelites and
stole their valuables, livestock, and crops. Most of the people of
Israel lived in constant fear hiding in caves and dens.

So there was Gideon hiding away threshing grain in a
winepress. Grain was usually threshed on the top of a hill so
the wind could blow away the chaff. But the situation in Israel
was so desperate that he had to thresh it down in a valley, hiding low in a winepress, hoping he would not be seen. Instead of

the wind blowing away the chaff, Gideon had to throw it into the air and hope a bit of it would blow away. No doubt such a position of weakness frustrated Gideon.

Then God's messenger appeared.

> *When the angel of the LORD appeared to Gideon, he said, "The LORD is with you, mighty warrior."*
>
> JUDGES 6:12

Just picture the irony of this: A grown man is hiding in a winepress when an angel of God appears and calls him "mighty warrior"! What was God doing? Bible commentators are divided on this point. Some say Gideon had a reputation as a warrior among the upper class of Israel.[1] Others say this is another example of God's great sense of humor.[2] Still others feel that "warrior" is a prophetic word describing Gideon's destiny.

I think that all three are true. Yes, God does have a wonderful sense of humor, but later events would indicate that Gideon did indeed have a background in battle. At the time Israel had no leader to lead them to rise up and fight. So Gideon was, for the time being, deprived of his destiny.

God's call beckoned to Gideon, showing him what he could and would be. I imagine that while Gideon was threshing grain he was thinking that Israel needed a leader to lead them out of this horrible state of humiliation. In his heart was a passion to be that deliverer. Now God had come to tell him that He wanted him to fulfill his destiny.

However, because the situation in Israel kept getting worse, Gideon was understandably hesitant to accept his mission. Even so, God was insistent. Let's listen in on their conversation.

> *"But sir," Gideon replied, "if the LORD is with us, why
> has all this happened to us? Where are all his wonders
> that our fathers told us about when they said, 'Did not
> the LORD bring us up out of Egypt?' But now the LORD
> has abandoned us and put us into the hand of Midian."*
>
> *The LORD turned to him and said, "Go in the
> strength you have and save Israel out of Midian's hand.
> Am I not sending you?"*
>
> *"But LORD," Gideon asked, "how can I save Israel?
> My clan is the weakest in Manasseh, and I am the least
> in my family."*
>
> *The LORD answered, "I will be with you, and you
> will strike down all the Midianites together."*
>
> JUDGES 6:13–16

God's call was clear: "Go and save Israel. I am sending you!"
Gideon was almost convinced, but it is highly unusual to have
the angel of the Lord call you to save a nation. He just wasn't sure
if God really was calling him to such a big task. Gideon needed
more. He needed a clear sign of confirmation.

I am so glad this story is in the Bible. We are a lot like Gideon. We want to hear God, to believe, to step out. But we don't
trust ourselves. We just aren't sure. Is it really God? Is this really
what God is saying?

This story is in the Bible not because Gideon wrestled with
confirmation, but because he used the situation to pray one of
the most effective prayers. Here is Gideon's simple prayer.

> *Gideon replied, "If now I have found favor in your eyes,
> give me a sign that it is really you talking to me."*
>
> JUDGES 6:17

### Give me a sign.

He was saying, "Make it clear. There is too much at risk. I am headed for absolute failure unless this is of You. I need confirmation. I have to know that I am not going crazy or having delusions of grandeur or volunteering for certain suicide. So, please, give me a sign."

Although some Bible teachers and pastors frown upon asking God for a sign, I think that there are those rare occasions in everyone's life when it is perfectly appropriate. Like Gideon, you sense God is calling you to something far greater, vastly higher, and much more difficult than you can imagine. You are making the biggest decision of your life. You are mostly convinced that you have heard His voice. But you have to be certain. The stakes are unbelievably high. You need confirmation.

Did God balk at Gideon and tell him that his request was foolish and immature? Let's find out.

> *"Please do not go away until I come back and bring my offering and set it before you." And the* LORD *said, "I will wait until you return."*
>
> *Gideon went in, prepared a young goat, and from an ephah of flour he made bread without yeast. Putting the meat in a basket and its broth in a pot, he brought them out and offered them to him under the oak.*
>
> *The angel of God said to him, "Take the meat and the unleavened bread, place them on this rock, and pour out the broth." And Gideon did so.*
>
> JUDGES 6:18–20

The stage was set for God to give Gideon his needed confirmation.

*With the tip of the staff that was in his hand, the angel of the LORD touched the meat and the unleavened bread. Fire flared from the rock, consuming the meat and the bread. And the angel of the LORD disappeared. When Gideon realized that it was the angel of the LORD, he exclaimed, "Ah, Sovereign LORD! I have seen the angel of the LORD face to face!"*

*But the LORD said to him, "Peace! Do not be afraid. You are not going to die." So Gideon built an altar to the LORD there and called it The LORD is Peace.*

JUDGES 6:21–24

Maybe you are facing a high-risk, high-reward venture. It could be that you sense God is speaking, but you aren't certain. You need to know exactly what He is saying. You need confirmation before you launch into this big decision.

Like you, my friend Rich needed such a sign. Here is his encouraging story.

*I had been praying for several years about whether the Lord wanted me to leave my job as a business law professor at OSU [the Ohio State University] and begin vocational ministry as the first senior pastor of our new church. I was bi-vocational, preaching many Sundays, leading several small groups, discipling a few men, and so on. In addition, I was a young professor working toward tenure, writing articles in scholarly journals, and authoring a textbook. My wife and I had two small children. Obviously the strain was pretty great.*

*I went to England to participate on a prayer ministry team at a conference. One Sunday evening I was speaking to a friend about my uncertainty regarding hearing God's voice. I said, "Kevin, I've been praying about whether God is calling me to full-time ministry for a number of years, but I'm no closer to knowing God's will now than I was four years ago. And I'm not interested in simply volunteering for something that God may not be calling me to."*

*Kevin, said, "Rich, why don't you ask the Lord for a sign?"*

*I responded, "I used to do that when I was a young Christian, but I think that is an immature way to seek God's will."*

*Kevin responded and said, "You know, Rich, every pastor in the world kicks poor Gideon around. But God didn't kick Gideon around. God is more than willing to meet you and give you the confirmation you need."*

*I thought, that's right. God was kind and gracious to Gideon. So that night I prayed, "Lord, if you want me to leave my job at OSU and pursue full-time ministry, please speak to me before Wednesday evening when I call my wife." I didn't prescribe how God was to speak to me, only that God simply would speak to me. I said, "Lord, if you don't speak to me before Wednesday night, I'll assume You are happy with what I'm doing and I just need to cut back on the number of hours that I'm devoting to church work."*

*Monday and Tuesday I heard nothing. On Wednesday evening I sat down at a two thousand-person conference. The speaker began his talk this way: "I was going to speak about healing tonight, but I feel like the Holy Spirit has instructed me to give a different message. I'm going to speak*

*about 'The Pearl of Great Price.'" He continued, saying,
"Some of you tonight are wondering if God is calling you
to full-time ministry. You will know it's the Lord when
it is the last hour, when there is no more time—then you
will know it's God."*

*I literally began squeezing the handrails of my chair.
I thought, Lord, are You speaking to me? It was literally the last hour before I was going to talk with my wife,
Marlene. In the course of the speaker's talk, he said seven
specific things that would happen when you know it's
time to move from your job into full-time ministry. All of
those things applied to my life.*

*The next day someone walked by me, turned around
and walked by again, and then turned around again.
He finally looked me in the eye and put his hand on my
chest and said, "The Lord is calling you to be a pastor."
There were several other remarkable confirmations in the
ensuing days that allowed me to know clearly and unmis-
takably that God had called me to leave my position at
Ohio State and go into full-time ministry.*[3]

## Making It Personal

I don't believe God will or should give us signs about every
little aspect of our lives. Before asking, there are several consid-
erations to take into account.

1. *All of us will probably need a sign of confirmation at one time
or another.* The need for a sign occurs rarely in a lifetime. Biblical
accounts of people receiving signs of confirmation almost always
revolve around a calling to a challenging ministry.

2. *God's signs often come at desperate times.* Israel was desperate for a deliverer. Gideon was desperate for a change.

3. *God's signs confirm what God is already doing or has already done in our hearts.* Signs may appear to come out of the blue. But a deeper look almost always reveals that God's callings and confirmations involve dreams and destinies that He has been writing on our hearts for a long time.

4. *Every sign should be checked against and submitted to the clear teachings of God's Word.* This seems obvious but needs to be stated. God will not give you a sign telling you to divorce your husband, have an affair with your secretary, or plunge your family into backbreaking debt. How do I know? Because the Bible tells me so.

5. *God can give us confirmation.* God is infinite. He can do whatever needs to be done. If you must have a sign of confirmation, He can give it. When I sensed God's call on my life to go into full-time ministry as a vocation, I had a preaching opportunity and asked God to give me confirmation. When nearly half the audience dedicated their lives to God, I knew that was my sign of confirmation.

Do you need clear confirmation that the direction you are heading is what God is calling you to do? Do as Gideon did. Ask God to give you a sign.

## NOTES

[1]Arthur Lewis, *Judges and Ruth* (Chicago, IL: Moody Press, 1979), p. 45.

[2]J. Vernon McGee, *Joshua and Judges* (Nashville: Thomas Nelson Publishers, 1991), p. 151.

[3]Used by permission of Rich Nathan, senior pastor of Vineyard Church, Columbus, Ohio.

# REMEMBER ME:

## The Prayer of Hannah

1 SAMUEL 1:11

Etched into every soul are deep, personal desires and dreams that refuse to go away until they are realized. We may temporarily lose sight of them in the busyness of day-to-day living, but they are always there, crying to be fulfilled. As time goes by, these yearnings take on a painful desperation when the hope of realizing them begins to fade. Nothing we or anyone can do, and no amount of time, can release us from the gnawing hurt of an unfulfilled dream. Doubts and questions disturb our prayers. You wonder, *Has God forgotten me?*

What can we do with these dreams that stubbornly refuse to come true and yet mulishly refuse to go away? We may want to try Hannah's prayer. Like all stories of great answers to prayer, this one begins with a great need. Hannah was a woman who needed nothing less than a miracle.

> *There was a certain man from Ramathaim, a Zuphite*
> *from the hill country of Ephraim, whose name was*
> *Elkanah son of Jeroham, the son of Elihu, the son of*
> *Tohu, the son of Zuph, an Ephraimite. He had two*
> *wives; one was called Hannah and the other Peninnah.*

*Peninnah had children, but Hannah had none. Year
after year this man went up from his town to worship
and sacrifice to the* LORD *Almighty at Shiloh, where
Hophni and Phinehas, the two sons of Eli, were priests of
the* LORD.

1 SAMUEL 1:1–3

Note the lonely, desperate, painful words at the end of verse
two: "Peninnah had children, but Hannah had none." Hannah
had no children in a world in which bearing children served as
the chief source of a woman's esteem, provision, and protection. Her arms had never felt the trembling joy of holding her
own baby. Her lifelong passion to be a mother went unfulfilled
year after year.

*Year after year this man went up from his town to wor-
ship and sacrifice to the* LORD *Almighty at Shiloh, where
Hophni and Phinehas, the two sons of Eli, were priests
of the* LORD. *Whenever the day came for Elkanah to
sacrifice, he would give portions of the meat to his wife
Peninnah and to all her sons and daughters. But to Hannah he gave a double portion because he loved her, and
the* LORD *had closed her womb. And because the* LORD
*had closed her womb, her rival kept provoking her in
order to irritate her. This went on year after year. Whenever Hannah went up to the house of the* LORD, *her rival
provoked her till she wept and would not eat. Elkanah
her husband would say to her, "Hannah, why are you
weeping? Why don't you eat? Why are you downhearted?
Don't I mean more to you than ten sons?"*

1 SAMUEL 1:3–8

"The Lord had closed her womb." As years passed, Hannah's barrenness caused her to become the object of scorn. And not only that, but she had a husband who totally misunderstood her pain. Like most men, Elkanah failed to understand why he wasn't the alpha and omega of his wife's desires.

Out of her desperation Hannah crafted a prayer, one of the most effective recorded in the Bible.

> *In bitterness of soul Hannah wept much and prayed to the* LORD. *And she made a vow, saying, "O* LORD *Almighty, if you will only look upon your servant's misery and remember me, and not forget your servant but give her a son, then I will give him to the* LORD *for all the days of his life, and no razor will ever be used on his head."*
>
> 1 SAMUEL 1:10–11

Do not miss the urgent simplicity of her prayer. It is summed up in those two anguished words, "Remember me."

### Remember me.

This desire to have a child was not a spur of the moment thing. The passion for parenthood grew daily in the womb of Hannah's soul. Undoubtedly, she tried other mothers' suggestions for how to get pregnant but with no success. She was getting older. Her biological clock was running or had run out. She was frantic for some action, some type of answer, a response from God.

Obviously this was not the first time she had prayed about her barrenness. Year after year she had made the trip to Shiloh. Yet her urgency now fused a yearningly specific request: "Remember me, and do not forget your servant, but give her a son." She did not merely seek *any* blessing. She was not even asking for *a* child. Hannah hammered heaven for a *son*.

I don't want to read too much into this prayer, but I sense that Hannah was a woman who wanted to touch a nation. She wanted to restore Israel to a right relationship with God. Her petition for a son was forged over the course of years in the fires of silence and frustration. Now her demand was clear. There was no other way. She had to have a son.

You see, in Hannah's Israel the odds of a woman, especially a barren wife, having such a national impact were slim. But a son, given to God, could grow to exercise prophetic power that could help prod a wayward people back to loving God.

So she cried out for a son. And, finally, God responded.

## Making It Personal

Before we look at God's answer, notice a few characteristics of this prayer. These elements could be understood as aids to answered prayers.

1. *Purified Motives.* One benefit of delayed answers is purified motives. The longer our dreams are heated in the flames of frustrating delay, the more the impurities in our motives are burned off. After years of yearning, Hannah's request had been refined to a sheen that God could no longer deny.

Her motives were pure. If or when God should give her a son, she promised to "give him to the Lord." She wanted this to be a God thing. God would be the giver and receiver of the son. The son would come from God and be returned to God. She merely wanted to have a part in the middle.

Yes, there was some "self" involved. Few of our deepest dreams and most passionate prayers are void of self. But while self was acknowledged, God was preeminent.

Hannah's dream was deeper than holding a baby. It reached further than herself, or her family, or even her village. She dreamed of a son, given by God, given back to God, who could be used of God to influence a nation for God.

These are the motives God blesses.

2. *Persistent Faith.*

> *As she kept on praying to the LORD, Eli observed her mouth.*
>
> 1 SAMUEL 1:12

Hannah's desperate desire was not merely offered to God once and forgotten. No, her prayer was repeated over and over as she bared her soul before her God.

In this regard, Hannah reminds me of the mistreated widow that Jesus spoke of in the Gospel of Luke.[1] Like Hannah, she had no choice. She was desperate and she was determined. Day after day, she came to the one with power, in this case a judge, and sought relief. She was shameless and stubborn. She was persistent and persevering. And eventually she prevailed. Her shameless and stubborn persistence won out. Jesus said He told this story to teach us that we should always pray and not give up. Then He remarked about the quality of faith displayed by the widow.

Like the widow, Hannah prayed and did not give up. Her faith refused to yield until it was rewarded.

3. *Painful Earnestness.*

> *Hannah was praying in her heart, and her lips were moving but her voice was not heard. Eli thought she was drunk and said to her, "How long will you keep on getting drunk? Get rid of your wine." "Not so, my lord," Hannah replied,*

*"I am a woman who is deeply troubled. I have not been drinking wine or beer; I was pouring out my soul to the* Lord. *Do not take your servant for a wicked woman; I have been praying here out of my great anguish and grief."*

1 Samuel 1:13–16

Hannah described herself as "a woman who is deeply troubled." By this point she was desperate. No one or nothing else but God would do. And the possibility of God not coming through was more than she could bear. So she "poured her soul out to the Lord."

She was not merely pouring out words to the Lord. In fact, so profound was her desire that her voice was not even heard. She was pouring out her very soul. Hers was an extremely deep, highly personal, supremely intimate prayer.

She claimed to be praying "out of great anguish and grief." This prayer erupted from so deep within the depths of her soul that it hurt to let it out. It was born from an intensity that was beyond what words could utter.

There is something painful about exposing the subterranean reaches of our souls to God. To let down the drawbridge and leave our greatest dreams and passions standing naked before God is threatening at best and often agonizing. Even though Hannah was in anguish, she would not retreat. She was in earnest.

4. *Petitions with Fasting.*

*Eli answered, "Go in peace, and may the God of Israel grant you what you have asked of him." She said, "May your servant find favor in your eyes." Then she went her way and ate something, and her face was no longer downcast.*

1 Samuel 1:17–18

Hannah did not eat until she was assured that she had broken through. Obviously, she had been abstaining from food as part of her prayer. She was either so determined that she would not eat or so distraught she could not eat, but either way she was fasting.

There has been much written on fasting in recent years. I know from experience that if a situation or the Holy Spirit dictates abstinence from food as a part of prayer, then it is well worth fasting. Most of the greatest answers to prayer I have ever enjoyed have come out of times of prayer with fasting. And that was the result for Hannah.

> *Early the next morning they arose and worshiped before the LORD and then went back to their home at Ramah. Elkanah lay with Hannah his wife, and the LORD remembered her. So in the course of time Hannah conceived and gave birth to a son. She named him Samuel, saying, "Because I asked the LORD for him."*
>
> 1 SAMUEL 1:19–20

Hannah got her answer when God gave her a son. Samuel was dedicated to God and became one of Israel's greatest prophets. He also became a man mighty in prayer. His name, meaning "God heard," was a constant reminder that God had answered a desperate prayer.

About every five years on Mother's Day at my church, we teach Hannah's desperate prayer. As a result, barren women and couples go to a deeper level in their prayers. Soon things start to happen. Women who couldn't get pregnant find themselves "with child." Couples are led to adopt precious babies in need of a home. And prodigal kids come home.

A friend of mine named Rhonda had had no contact with her adult daughter, Megan, for several years. But a few years ago when Rhonda became a part of a church and, after decades of distance, returned to God, she discovered a renewed burden on her heart to connect with her daughter. One Sunday morning she heard a message on the power of prayer and fasting. After all the years of estrangement, Rhonda realized she had nothing to lose.

She began her fast on Monday and sought God with desperate prayer each day. On Thursday evening the telephone rang. It was Megan, calling to say she wanted to get together. God had remembered Rhonda.

But that's not all Rhonda prayed about. She began to pray about Megan's spiritual condition. Soon Megan began coming to church with her and recently accepted Christ as her Savior.[2]

I believe that God wants and is able to give us our deepest, "pure motive" desires. If you're burdened like Rhonda and Hannah, identify the deep, God-sized desire of your heart. Ask God for it persistently, earnestly, and honestly with fasting until you get a response. Of course, if the request is not for the best, God may not answer, or He may let you wait for a long stretch of time until your motives are purified. But if your desire is God given, and God purified, then watch out. You may be given your own "Samuel" to give back to the Lord so that He might bless others.

## NOTES

[1]Luke 18:1–7.

[2]Used by permission of Rhonda Tucker.

# I HAVE SINNED:

*The Prayer of David*

2 SAMUEL 12:13

You remember what David did. It was ugly. In the midst of his midlife season, bored and weary, he opted out of responsibility (1 Samuel 11:1). And then, with his defenses down, he foolishly initiated an illicit sexual encounter with a married woman named Bathsheba. When she became pregnant (11:2–5), David desperately tried to hide his sin under a blanket of deception. It failed because, ironically, Bathsheba's husband, Uriah, displayed the character and commitment that David lacked (11:6–13). Frantically and decisively, David blatantly misused his power to have Uriah killed in battle (11:14–26). He then married Bathsheba, assuming "no one would ever know." But David knew—and God always knows.

Know that guilt follows sin like a vulture attaches itself to rotten meat. Guilt followed David because he had sinned. His record now carried the heinous stains of adultery, deception, misuse of authority, and murder.

If anyone knew better, it was David. David knew God does not tolerate such behavior. Carefully read these words from the pen of David:

*You are not a God who takes pleasure in evil; with you
the wicked cannot dwell.*

PSALM 5:4

*God is a righteous judge, a God who expresses his wrath
every day.*

PSALM 7:11

*The LORD examines the righteous, but the wicked and
those who love violence his soul hates. On the wicked he
will rain fiery coals and burning sulfur; a scorching wind
will be their lot. For the LORD is righteous, he loves jus-
tice; upright men will see his face.*

PSALM 11:5–7

*LORD, who may dwell in your sanctuary? Who may live on
your holy hill? He whose walk is blameless and who does
what is righteous, who speaks the truth from his heart and
has no slander on his tongue, who does his neighbor no
wrong and casts no slur on his fellowman. . .but the Lord
laughs at the wicked, for he knows their day is coming. . .
the offspring of the wicked will be cut off.*

PSALM 15:1–3; 37:13, 28

Earlier, David had even boasted of his blameless living on
more than one occasion. How hollow and haunting these words
must have been in the face of his guilt!

*Hear, O LORD, my righteous plea; listen to my cry. Give
ear to my prayer—it does not rise from deceitful lips.
May my vindication come from you; may your eyes see*

*what is right. Though you probe my heart and examine me at night, though you test me, you will find nothing; I have resolved that my mouth will not sin. As for the deeds of men—by the word of your lips I have kept myself from the ways of the violent. My steps have held to your paths; my feet have not slipped.*

PSALM 17:1–5

*Vindicate me, O LORD, for I have led a blameless life; I have trusted in the LORD without wavering. . . . I walk continually in your truth. I do not sit with deceitful men.*

PSALM 26:1, 3–4

David lived a year under intense and immense guilt. As hell is the expression of the absence of God, and guilt excludes us from the presence of God, David's year was a living hell. David later described the agony of his year of distance through disobedience. Feel the misery contained in these words:

*I am faint. . .for my bones are in agony. My soul is in anguish. . .I am worn out from groaning; all night long I flood my bed with weeping and drench my couch with tears.*

PSALM 6:2–3, 6

*When I kept silent, my bones wasted away through my groaning all day long. For day and night your hand was heavy upon me; my strength was sapped as in the heat of summer.*

PSALM 32:3–4

*Your arrows have pierced me, and your hand has come down upon me. . . . There is no health in my body; my*

*bones have no soundness because of my sin. My guilt*
*has overwhelmed me like a burden too heavy to bear.*
*My wounds fester and are loathsome because of my sin-*
*ful folly. I am bowed down and brought very low; all*
*day long I go about mourning. My back is filled with*
*searing pain; there is no health in my body. I am feeble*
*and utterly crushed; I groan in anguish of heart. . . . I*
*am like a deaf man, who cannot hear, like a mute, who*
*cannot open his mouth. . . . For I am about to fall, and*
*my pain is ever with me.*

PSALM 38:2–8, 13, 17

Guilt is horrible, hideous, terrible, and terrifying. Yet, God is merciful. He does not abandon us to be swallowed in the cesspool of our guilt. Instead, He pursues us. His Spirit haunts us. His Word hunts us down and speaks to us.

God's love, His Spirit, and words of rebuke chased David down. The messenger's name was Nathan. Nathan told David a story that touched his sense of injustice and provoked him to demand punishment for a thieving sinner (2 Samuel 12:1–6). Then Nathan skillfully turned the tables on David and cut him straight to the heart with four chilling words: "You are the man" (2 Samuel 12:7).

God always convicts in specifics. Satan accuses in generalities. Nathan did not have to be specific with David. God already had done that. David knew exactly what Nathan meant. David was caught. He could hide no longer.

At this point David had three choices: throw Nathan out, deny his guilt, or own it. To his credit, David immediately said the only words that can erase the awful stains of guilt: "I have sinned against the Lord" (2 Samuel 12:23).

**I have sinned.**

"I have sinned." So states one of the most effective—and one of the most difficult—prayers recorded in the Bible. Pride hates to admit weakness, and arrogance dislikes acknowledging short-comings. Just ask Adam and Eve. Rather than owning their sin, Adam blamed God and Eve blamed the serpent. But God knew the truth (Genesis 3:8–13).

I have found that when God convicts us of sin, the easi-est thing to say is "yes." Silence, excuses, rationalization, and deflection don't work. Forgiveness comes through confession.

After David admitted his sin, grace and mercy were spilled out in his behalf. Immediately, Nathan spoke the best words a guilty soul can ever hear when he said, "The Lord has taken away your sin" (2 Samuel 12:13).

What sweet, glorious, mighty words those were for David, and are to us! The Lord has taken away your guilt. What liberat-ing, life-giving words! Our God is the God who forgives sin and erases guilt.

Slowly read these promises and thank God for His astound-ing mercy:

> *"Come now, let us reason together," says the LORD.*
> *"Though your sins are like scarlet, they shall be as white*
> *as snow; though they are red as crimson, they shall be*
> *like wool."*
>
> ISAIAH 1:18

> *"I, even I, am he who blots out your transgressions, for*
> *my own sake, and remembers your sins no more."*
>
> ISAIAH 43:25

*Let the wicked forsake his way and the evil man his thoughts. Let him turn to the LORD, and he will have mercy on him, and to our God, for he will freely pardon.*

ISAIAH 55:7

*If we confess our sins, he is faithful and just and will forgive us our sins and purify us from all unrighteousness.*

1 JOHN 1:9

*Who is a God like you, who pardons sin and forgives the transgression of the remnant of his inheritance? You do not stay angry forever but delight to show mercy. You will again have compassion on us; you will tread our sins underfoot and hurl all our iniquities into the depths of the sea.*

MICAH 7:18–19

*For as high as the heavens are above the earth, so great is his love for those who fear him; as far as the east is from the west, so far has he removed our transgressions from us.*

PSALM 103:11–12

In high school I had a friend who was slow to accept the truth, love, and mercy of God. She said that she had intellectual obstacles to faith. But more importantly, she had an incident of immorality in her past for which she felt guilty and ashamed. She doubted that God would fully forgive her.

Eventually the testimony of spiritually turned-on believers and the persistent pursuit of the love of God wore her down. She relented and ran home to the Father. She found His arms wide open and His mercy to be mighty.

"It felt so very good to be forgiven," she told me the next

day. "It was like I was a little girl in a new clean dress dancing in a refreshing spring shower." Her face erupted into a magnificent smile as she gushed, "I have never felt so incredibly clean!"

David knew exactly what she meant. It's no wonder that he wrote these words:

> *Blessed is he whose transgressions are forgiven, whose sins are covered. Blessed is the man whose sin the LORD does not count against him and in whose spirit is no deceit. . . . I acknowledged my sin to you and did not cover up my iniquity. I said, "I will confess my transgressions to the LORD"—and you forgave the guilt of my sin.*
>
> PSALM 32:1–2, 5

After his confession and forgiveness, David's God-given eloquence was unleashed. Read the urgent words of his prayer.

> *Have mercy on me, O God, according to your unfailing love; according to your great compassion blot out my transgressions. Wash away all my iniquity and cleanse me from my sin. . . .*
>
> *Cleanse me with hyssop, and I will be clean; wash me, and I will be whiter than snow. Let me hear joy and gladness; let the bones you have crushed rejoice. Hide your face from my sins and blot out all my iniquity.*
>
> *Create in me a pure heart, O God, and renew a steadfast spirit within me. Do not cast me from your presence or take your Holy Spirit from me. Restore to me the joy of your salvation and grant me a willing spirit, to sustain me.*
>
> *Then I will teach transgressors your ways, and sinners*

*will turn back to you. Save me from bloodguilt, O God, the God who saves me, and my tongue will sing of your righteousness. O Lord, open my lips, and my mouth will declare your praise.*

*You do not delight in sacrifice, or I would bring it; you do not take pleasure in burnt offerings. The sacrifices of God are a broken spirit; a broken and contrite heart, O God, you will not despise.*

PSALM 51:1–2, 7–17

## Making It Personal

I don't know what sin or sins you need to confess to God right now. Maybe it's something you said or did. It could be an attitude you have developed or a thought you have had. Maybe it's something you know you should do but haven't, for whatever reason. Don't argue with God. If He is putting His finger on a specific sin or sins in your life, the time to confess is now. Don't wait any longer. Pray the prayer of David, "I have sinned."

# ENLARGE MY TERRITORY:

## *The Prayer of Jabez*

### 1 CHRONICLES 4:10

"Surely I was born for more than this."

Sound familiar? Have you ever had a gnawing hunger and restless burden of wanting to do more and be more for God? If so, you are not alone. You were created with the craving to do your part to create a better world.

God is the fulfiller of dreams. I believe that at conception He begins writing dreams on each of our hearts. These deep dreams perfectly wed His purposes on the planet with the passion of our souls. In your heart today are the seeds of great imaginings of a future you hope for, long for, and dream of either consciously or subconsciously. God planted them there. They are the secret of your fulfillment.

One man took a risk and acted on his ambition. His name was Jabez, and his story has been widely publicized recently in Christian circles. Interestingly, the Bible record of Jabez is condensed into four short sentences found in two simple verses.

*Jabez was more honorable than his brothers. His mother*
*had named him Jabez, saying, "I gave birth to him in*
*pain." Jabez cried out to the God of Israel, "Oh, that*

*you would bless me and enlarge my territory! Let
your hand be with me, and keep me from harm so
that I will be free from pain." And God granted his
request.*

1 CHRONICLES 4:9–10

God summarized the entire life of Jabez into four facts:
(1) Jabez was more honorable than his brothers; (2) He
received his name, Jabez, because his mother gave birth to
him in pain; (3) He asked God to give him his dream of en-
larged territory; and (4) God answered, "Yes!" Jabez's prayer is
one of the most effective prayers in the Bible. We are not told
*how* God answered, but we are clearly told *that* God granted
his request.

Likewise, Jabez's request was fourfold: (1) Bless me; (2)
Enlarge my territory; (3) Let Your hand be with me; and (4)
Keep me from harm so that I will be free from pain.

Of the four requests made by Jabez, the one I find most com-
pelling is "enlarge my territory," because I find myself yearning
for the same thing. But is it selfish or arrogant to ask God for
that? The first time I read this verse, I assumed that God would
say, "You have got to be kidding!"

But God took the sincere cry of Jabez's heart seriously. So,
I figure, if God would do such a thing for Jabez, He might do
it for me. And He has.

### Enlarge my territory.

Asking God to enlarge our territory is not something we should
feel guilty about. It can leave a powerful testimony with the
world, according to Henry Blackaby.

*God is interested in the world coming to know him. The
only way people will know him is when they see him at
work. Whenever God involves you in his activity, the
assignment will have God-like dimensions to it. Some
people say, "God will never ask me to do something I
can't do." I have come to the place in my life that, if the
assignment I sense God is giving me is something I can
handle, I know it probably is not from God. The kind of
assignments God gives. . .are always beyond what people
can do because he wants to demonstrate his nature, his
strength, his provision, and his kindness to his people
and to a watching world. That is the only way the world
will come to know him. . . . When God's people and the
world see something happen that only God can do, they
come to know Him.*[1]

When we ask God to enlarge our territory, we are asking
God to increase our sphere of influence for His kingdom.
Bruce Wilkinson helps us understand how this prayer works.

*If Jabez had worked on Wall Street, he might have
prayed, "Lord increase the value of my investments/port-
folios." When I talk to presidents of companies, I often
talk to them in terms of this particular mind-set. When
Christian executives ask me, "Is it right for me to ask
for more business?" my response is, "Absolutely!" If you're
doing business God's way, it's not only right to ask for
more, but He is waiting for you to ask. Your business is
God's territory that God has entrusted to you. He wants
you to accept it as a significant opportunity to touch individual lives, the business community, and the world for*

*His glory. Asking Him to enlarge that opportunity brings Him only delight.*[2]

When we ask for more territory we are tapping into the heart of Jesus, whose heart was so large it encompassed the whole world. Among His final words to His followers was to "make disciples of *all* nations" (Matthew 28:19); to "preach the good news to *all* creation" (Mark 16:15); that "repentance and forgiveness of sins be preached in his name to *all* nations" (Luke 24:47); and for His followers to be His "witnesses in Jerusalem, and in *all* Judea and Samaria, and to the ends of the earth" (Acts 1:8) [all italics are mine]. Notice the word "all" in each reference. Part of the world was not enough. Some of the people won't do. He wanted His kingdom, His territory, to extend to *all* the people in the world.

When we ask God to expand our territory we are standing on the shoulders of spiritual giants. At the age of eighty-five Joshua's visionary buddy Caleb was not ready to retire, nor was he content with the status quo. He asked for greater territory.

*"So here I am today, eighty-five years old! I am still as strong today as the day Moses sent me out; I'm just as vigorous to go out to battle now as I was then. Now give me this hill country that the* Lord *promised me that day."*

JOSHUA 14:10–12

Enlarge my territory is a prayer God loves to answer. John Knox, the great fifteenth-century Scottish reformer prayed, "Give me Scotland or I will die!" He almost succeeded. Even though he was unsuccessful in his attempt to win Mary, Queen of Scots, to Christ, she is reputed to have said, "I fear the prayers of John Knox more than all the assembled armies of Europe."

Likewise, Henrietta Mears was a big dreamer. At the age of thirty-eight she took the position of director of Christian education at the First Presbyterian Church in Hollywood, California. "God doesn't call us to sit on the sidelines and watch. He calls us to be on the field, playing the games," said Ms. Mears. Knowing Christ intimately and telling others about Him was her first and foremost objective.

Three years after her arrival at the church, Sunday school attendance grew from four hundred to four thousand. During her tenure over four hundred young people entered full-time Christian service. One of them was Bill Bright, founder of Campus Crusade for Christ.

God kept expanding her territory. Frustrated with the material being taught in the Sunday school when she arrived, she began to write lessons that would honor Christ and be faithful to the Bible. It wasn't long before her efforts gained results and requests for copies of her material came in from all across the country. Her office staff worked many long hours mimeographing and mailing the lessons. When the demand became too great, Mears and a group of businesspeople established Gospel Light Publications, one of the first publishers in the Christian education field.

For years, Mears searched for a retreat area where she could take her high-school and college-aged students. She asked God to provide for her dream. Soon, a privately owned resort in the San Bernardino Mountains was available, but the price was too high. For a moment, the dream appeared impossible. Mears called a group of people together for prayer. She insisted that they should "dream big whenever God was involved" and trust Him for His blessing at the right time. After a miraculous intervention, Forest Home, valued at $350,000, was purchased in 1938 for the unheard of price of $30,000.

God expanded her territory into unique realms. Initially, Mears had been drawn to California for the opportunity to witness to those in the entertainment industry. God provided an open door into this area through the Hollywood Christian Group, which began meeting in her home. Many entertainment professionals came to know Christ as a result of her ministry. Dozens of Christian leaders acknowledge her as well, including Billy Graham who said of her, "I doubt if any other woman outside my wife and mother has had such a marked influence [on my life]."[3]

And the stories of such trust in God continue!

In 1931 a young man decided to pray two hours a day every morning for forty days before he went to work. He took a map with him as he lay on his face before God in prayer in the Sierra Nevada Mountains of California. By the end of a few weeks he was asking God to extend his spiritual influence to every state in the United States. As his burden and his faith grew, he was asking for continents he could touch by "training trainers of men."

God heard his cry. By the beginning of World War II, the young man, Dawson Trotman, and his resulting organization, The Navigators, had raised up "key men" for every ship in the United States Navy. Because of the war, Trotman's ministry was extending around the world.

A few years later, Trotman died the way he had lived— saving others. At the age of fifty he went home to be with the Lord after rescuing someone from a cold lake. At his funeral Billy Graham said, "I think he touched more lives than any man I have ever known. We today represent thousands of people touched by this great man."

Graham continued, "Dawson was a man of vision. When our God is small, the world looks big; but when our God is big, the world looks small. And Dawson saw the world as conquerable for Christ. To Dawson, God was big and the world was little. The day he went to be with the Lord some of his men arrived from Africa. One of his great visions was to open Africa. He was always dreaming, planning, and scheming about new ways and means of reaching people."

Trotman was constantly asking God for new ground. He surely was a student and practitioner of the prayer of Jabez when he effectively asked God to "enlarge my territory." The ministry he started, The Navigators, is guiding tens of thousands of people worldwide to come to know and grow in Jesus Christ. Internationally, more than 3,800 Navigators of 62 nationalities serve in more than 100 countries.[4]

### Making It Personal

What is the dream God has etched into your soul? Is it seeing your children become great Christians? Starting your own business? Becoming a nurse? Building a great church? Training teens? Writing a Christian bestseller? Winning your family to Christ? If God could expand the territory of Jabez, He can expand yours.

## NOTES

[1] Henry Blackaby and Claude King, *Experiencing God* (Nashville, TN: Broadman and Holman, 1995), p. 138. Used by permission.

[2] Bruce Wilkinson, *The Prayer of Jabez* (Sisters, OR: Multnomah Publishers, 2000), pp. 31–32.

[3] "Henrietta Mears: Dream Big," In Touch Ministries, www.intouch.org/myintouch/mighty/portraits/henrietta mears 213642.

[4] "Dawson Trotman: The Disciplined Life," In Touch Ministries, www.intouch.org/myintouch/mighty/portraits/dawson trotman 213713.

## 8

# GIVE ME WISDOM:
## *The Prayer of Solomon*
### 2 CHRONICLES 1:10

What if God gave you the sweetest deal of the century? Maybe the best offer in the millennium? Suppose God said to you, "Ask Me for whatever you want and I will give it to you."

Can you imagine? "Ask Me for *whatever* you want—anything at all, nothing is too big—*and I will,* not might, or could, but I will *give it to you.*"

What would you ask for? Would it be truckloads of money (not to be used selfishly, of course)? Would you want to be able to pay off your bills, help out some friends, secure your children's future, help your church, support a bunch of missionaries, and pay for finding a cure for cancer or AIDS? It may cross your mind that having a new house and luxury car might be a way to let people know that God is not a stingy God. After all, it's okay to have money as long as it doesn't have you.

Or would you go for an ultimate makeover? Would you want a younger, sleeker, stronger, healthier model? Maybe you desire a tall, blond, and beautiful version, or would you ask for the tall, dark, and handsome edition? Of course, the reason you would want this wonder body would be so you could share your faith more confidently and serve the Lord more effectively.

The Prayer of Solomon

Or, you might ask for some super powers. Think of all the
people you could help if you could heal crowds of sick people as
Jesus did. Raising the dead certainly could glorify God. Feeding
thousands with a small boy's lunch is a beneficial ability.

Hearing God tell you that He would gladly give you anything
you asked would be a mind-boggling prospect. Impossible, you
say? Not so. Nearly three thousand years ago, God gave that exact
opportunity to a man named Solomon (1 Chronicles 1:7).

Solomon had his hands full. As the second son of the fateful David and Bathsheba union, he was born with a stain on his
record. His home life wasn't easy with five stepmothers and some
wild half-brothers. One half-brother, Amnon, raped his half-
sister, Tamar. Her brother, Absalom, then sought revenge and
murdered Amnon (2 Samuel 13). Later, Absalom made a violent,
and ultimately suicidal, play for the throne (2 Samuel 14–18).

Yet, Solomon was to be given the reins of the kingdom of
his father, King David. David was the action superhero of 1000
BC. He was good looking, dashing, intelligent, hugely talented,
and a larger-than-life living legend. He was a man's man and a
ladies' man, and yet he was a man after God's own heart. David's
résumé reads like a fantasy. He was a boy shepherd, military
hero, gifted songwriter, folk legend, national spiritual leader, and
king. He had killed Goliath, eluded Saul's army, recruited a band
of merry men, become the king, led a tiny nation to become a
world power, written many Psalms, created the "Bathsheba-gate"
scandal, survived an ugly military coup plotted by his own son,
and he planned to build God a great temple.

When David died, the weight of a young nation rested on
the untested shoulders of his son, Solomon. He had to step up
and take David's place as king. Talk about big shoes to fill!

Yet, God knows when we are facing more than we can

handle, and He knows just what we need. So God appeared to Solomon in a dream and made him the unconditional proposal: "Ask Me for whatever you want and I will give it to you." To his credit, Solomon knew what to ask for.

> *That night God appeared to Solomon and said to him, "Ask for whatever you want me to give you." Solomon answered God, "You have shown great kindness to David my father and have made me king in his place. Now, LORD God, let your promise to my father David be confirmed, for you have made me king over a people who are as numerous as the dust of the earth. Give me wisdom and knowledge, that I may lead this people, for who is able to govern this great people of yours?"*
>
> 2 CHRONICLES 1:7–10

**Give me wisdom.**
Solomon asked for what he believed to be the most important gift anyone can receive—wisdom. He ranked wisdom ahead of money or looks or miracle powers.

Solomon was a diligent student and he used his time growing up in the court of a king to study from the greatest minds of his land. He accumulated the teachings of the ages and collected the parables of the sages. It was his conclusion that the road to blessing leads through the doorway of wisdom. In his book, Proverbs, he wrote the following:

> *Blessed is the man who finds wisdom, the man who gains understanding, for she is more profitable than silver and yields better returns than gold. She is more precious than rubies; nothing you desire can compare with her. Long*

*life is in her right hand; in her left hand are riches and honor. Her ways are pleasant ways, and all her paths are peace. She is a tree of life to those who embrace her; those who lay hold of her will be blessed.*

PROVERBS 3:13–18

To Solomon, if you can only acquire a single gift, the gift to get is wisdom.

*Get wisdom, get understanding; do not forget my words or swerve from them. Do not forsake wisdom, and she will protect you; love her, and she will watch over you.*

PROVERBS 4:5–6

In his mind, wisdom was life's most valuable pursuit.

*Wisdom is supreme; therefore get wisdom. Though it cost all you have, get understanding. Esteem her, and she will exalt you; embrace her, and she will honor you. She will set a garland of grace on your head and present you with a crown of splendor.*

PROVERBS 4:7–9

A careful study of the book of Proverbs reveals wisdom to be the diligently acquired art of skillful living. It is the careful cultivation of a God-centered, Christ-like, character-driven, common-sense way of living. Wisdom is the path that leads to God. It is characterized by righteousness, mercy, tact, humility, discipline, respect for authority, "teachability," and honesty.

So, when given the opportunity to ask God for anything, Solomon asked for wisdom. "Give me wisdom" is one of the most effective prayers found in the pages of Scripture, and one God loves to answer. The Book of 1 Kings records God's response.

> *The Lord was pleased that Solomon had asked for this.*
> *So God said to him, "Since you have asked for this and*
> *not for long life or wealth for yourself, nor have asked for*
> *the death of your enemies but for discernment in admin-*
> *istering justice, I will do what you have asked. I will give*
> *you a wise and discerning heart, so that there will never*
> *have been anyone like you, nor will there ever be."*
>
> 1 KINGS 3:10–12

In 2 Chronicles we read this record of the Lord's answer:

> *God said to Solomon, "Since this is your heart's desire and*
> *you have not asked for wealth, riches or honor, nor for the*
> *death of your enemies, and since you have not asked for*
> *a long life but for wisdom and knowledge to govern my*
> *people over whom I have made you king, therefore wisdom*
> *and knowledge will be given you. And I will also give you*
> *wealth, riches and honor, such as no king who was before*
> *you ever had and none after you will have."*
>
> 2 CHRONICLES 1:11–12

Soon after, Solomon's wisdom was put on display. Two harlots came to Solomon for a verdict. They both lived in the same house and both were mothers of newborn children. Woman number one claimed that woman number two's baby died in the night so woman number two switched babies while woman number one was still asleep. Woman number two denied it. It was up to Solomon to decide who was right.

Shrewdly he ordered a man to cut the living baby in half and give each woman a half. The first woman cried out, "Give her the baby. Don't kill him!" The second woman said, "Neither of us will have a living baby. Cut him in two."

The ploy worked perfectly. Solomon ordered, "Don't kill that baby. Give him to the first woman. She obviously is the real mother."[1] Not surprisingly, Solomon's reputation for unusual wisdom spread throughout the nation.

Solomon asked for wisdom and God said, "Yes." In the Book of 1 Kings we can read a summary of the amazing way God answered Solomon's prayer for wisdom.

*God gave Solomon wisdom and very great insight, and a breadth of understanding as measureless as the sand on the seashore. Solomon's wisdom was greater than the wisdom of all the men of the East, and greater than all the wisdom of Egypt. He was wiser than any other man, including Ethan the Ezrahite—wiser than Heman, Calcol and Darda, the sons of Mahol. And his fame spread to all the surrounding nations. He spoke three thousand proverbs and his songs numbered a thousand and five. He described plant life, from the cedar of Lebanon to the hyssop that grows out of walls. He also taught about animals and birds, reptiles and fish. Men of all nations came to listen to Solomon's wisdom, sent by all the kings of the world, who had heard of his wisdom.*

1 KINGS 4:29–33

Solomon became known as one of the wisest and richest men who ever lived. The "wisdom" books of the Bible—Proverbs, Song of Solomon, and Ecclesiastes—came from his divinely inspired pen. It was God who answered his prayer for wisdom.

Like Solomon, Jesus' adolescence and young adult years were characterized by progress in wisdom (Luke 2:52). If Jesus as a mortal being needed to grow in wisdom, how much more do you and I?

### Making It Personal

Asking God for wisdom and receiving it is not a one-time deal that only Solomon was able to cash in on. "Give me wisdom" is a prayer all of us can pray with confidence. The New Testament book of James gives us the encouragement to ask for wisdom with this promise: "If any of you lacks wisdom, he should ask God, who gives generously to all without finding fault, and *it will be given to him*" (James 1:5).

Of the twenty-one most effective prayers, the one I use most often is "Give me wisdom." I have three teenage sons and I lead a church. There is always a need to make an important decision or give someone necessary advice. I have learned to ask for wisdom and God is faithful to answer.

With what decisions are you currently wrestling? Do you need wisdom to carry out your ministry more effectively? Are you trying to figure out how to lead your family? Do you need insight into a relationship? Do your job responsibilities require you to make decisions that affect the livelihoods of other people? Are there other areas where you need wisdom?

When Solomon prayed, "Give me wisdom," God answered "Yes!" Pause right now and ask God to give you wisdom for every decision you are encountering and every situation you face today.

### NOTES

[1]See 1 Kings 3:16–28.

# ANSWER ME:

## *The Prayer of Elijah*

1 KINGS 18:37

Elijah needed a miracle. There are many times when what we need is an answer to prayer. And then there are those rare, probably once in a lifetime moments when we have to have a miracle. The Old Testament prophet did not need a nice, run of the mill, easily explainable answer to prayer. The situation demanded an outright, jaw-dropping, undeniable, superceding-the-laws-of-nature, impressive, verifiable miracle! Without it, Elijah would be killed and God's chosen people would drift into pagan oblivion.

As Charles Dickens would say, it was the worst of times. King Ahab and Queen Jezebel had steered the nation of Israel down a road leading away from the Lord and then stepped on the accelerator—and woe to anyone who caused a traffic jam! Ahab was a man whose wickedness was exceeded only by that of his wife, Jezebel. Everything about that woman dripped iniquity and emanated evil. Together, they publicly promoted the worship of the pagan god Baal.

In order to shock the nation back from its dangerous path, the Lord sent a drought. This was not just a seasonal sign but a heaven-sent plague that lasted for three long years. The lack of rain was an obvious slap in the face of the supposed rain god, Baal.

After three years without rain, the people stood precariously with one foot on either side, partially following the false god and sort of following the Lord. Not a good place to be.

Into this boiling cauldron of chaos, God sent His man, Elijah, the roughhewn prophet. He was a wild, eccentric, bold messenger of the Almighty God. Risking death, Elijah faced Ahab and challenged him to gather the people for a power duel of deities.

When the day of decision dawned, Elijah stood alone on Mt. Carmel facing 450 prophets of Baal and 400 prophets of the goddess Asherah before the gathered nation of Israel. The odds were 950 to 1. It looked like a mismatch. As it turned out, it was.

Sidestepping political correctness, Elijah confronted the people with a challenge: "Quit sitting on the fence! If the Lord is the real God, follow Him. If Baal is the one, follow him" (1 Kings 18:21, paraphrased).

The people sat in stunned silence as he continued, "Let's have a duel between the deities. We will both offer an ox on the altar. The Baal prophets will pray to their God, and I will pray to mine. The god who answers with fire will prove to be the real God. The winner takes all" (1 Kings 18:22–24, paraphrased).

Since Baal was supposedly able to control lightning, thunder, and rain, everyone agreed. Humans love to watch car wrecks. The show would be highly entertaining.

The Baal prophets went first. They prayed all morning, "Baal, answer us." The only response they received was a wall of absolute silence. When Elijah began to taunt them, they prayed louder, harder, and more passionately. They did anything they could think of to provoke a response from their deity. Yet, there was not even a flicker of a reply. They prayed all afternoon.

Nothing. Nada. Zippo. Baal had failed (see 1 Kings 18:27–29).

Then it was Elijah's turn. First, he repaired the altar the other prophets had knocked down in their feeble attempts to attract the attention of Baal. He dug a trench around the altar and then put wood on it and another ox. Then he did an absolutely outrageous thing. Elijah had the altar drenched in water, time after time, until the excess water filled the trench. He had to be crazy. If 950 prophets' prayers could not get their god to send a spark, how did he think one man could get his God to consume a water-soaked sacrifice?

Standing in front of the altar before an entire nation and the hundreds of false prophets and King Ahab, Elijah needed a miracle. If he failed, they would kill him, and the Lord would be squeezed out of the nation through Ahab's political clout.

So Elijah did the only thing a man in desperate need of an impossible miracle does. He prayed. How big is God? Big enough! So Elijah offered one of the most effective prayers recorded in the Bible and asked God for a really big thing:

> *At the time of sacrifice, the prophet Elijah stepped forward and prayed: "O LORD, God of Abraham, Isaac and Israel, let it be known today that you are God in Israel and that I am your servant and have done all these things at your command. Answer me, O LORD, answer me, so these people will know that you, O LORD, are God, and that you are turning their hearts back again."*
>
> 1 KINGS 18:36–37

**Answer me.**

Elijah offered a simple, two-word request, "Answer me." And God did.

> *Then the fire of the LORD fell and burned up the sacri-
> fice, the wood, the stones and the soil, and also licked up
> the water in the trench.*
>
> I KINGS 18:38

I read this story to my boys when they were little. One
gasped in glee and another looked around and said, "Whoa!"
The third one smiled and said, "Cool."

I would have loved to see the fire of the Lord shoot down
from heaven. Wouldn't it have been awesome to see the looks
on the faces of the people? What a blast to witness the humiliation and total embarrassment of the false prophets! Wouldn't it
have been sheer delight to see the frustrated anger on the wicked
king's face?

Elijah's petition was powerful. The prophets of Baal prayed
all day and Baal couldn't even make a spark to light dry kin-
dling wood. Then Elijah prayed for less than a minute and God
sent fire from heaven that was so mighty it ignited a soaking
wet sacrifice and burned up the wet wood, saturated stones,
and soil. And if that wasn't enough, the blaze consumed all the
water in the trench.

I say, "Wow!" And so did the people who witnessed the
miracle.

> *When all the people saw this, they fell prostrate and
> cried, "The LORD—he is God! The LORD—he is God!"*
>
> I KINGS 18:39

How big is God? Big enough!

The spiritual direction of an entire nation was turned back to
God all because one man was not afraid to confront the enemy

and ask God for a miracle. Elijah lived in the largeness of God, and miracles were the result. He prayed, "Answer me!" And God did. He prayed, "Answer me!" And many people were steered back on course. He asked for a victory-producing miracle, and the enemy was crushed.

Twenty-five years ago I had the privilege of hearing a wonderful woman speak. Helen Roseveare was a missionary doctor who spent twenty years ministering in the Congo. This was one of the awesome stories she told:

*One night I had worked hard to help a mother in the labor ward; but in spite of all we could do she died leaving us with a tiny premature baby and a crying two-year-old daughter. We would have difficulty keeping the baby alive, as we had no incubator. (We had no electricity to run an incubator.) We also had no special feeding facilities.*

*Although we lived on the equator, nights were often chilly with treacherous drafts. One student midwife went for the box we had for such babies and the cotton wool the baby would be wrapped in. Another went to stoke up the fire and fill a hot water bottle. She came back shortly in distress to tell me that in filling the bottle, it had burst. Rubber perishes easily in tropical climates. "And it is our last hot water bottle!" she exclaimed.*

*As in the West, it is no good crying over spilled milk, so in Central Africa it might be considered no good crying over burst water bottles. They do not grow on trees, and there are no drugstores down forest pathways.*

*"All right," I said, "put the baby near the fire as you safely can, and sleep between the baby and the door*

to keep it free from drafts. Your job is to keep the baby warm."

The following noon, as I did most days, I went to have prayers with any of the orphanage children who chose to gather with me. I gave the youngsters various suggestions of things to pray about and told them about the tiny baby. I explained our problem about keeping the baby warm enough, mentioning the hot water bottle. The baby could so easily die if it got chills. I also told them of the two-year-old sister, crying because her mother had died. During the prayer time, one ten-year-old girl, Ruth, prayed with the usual blunt conciseness of our African children. "Please, God," she prayed, "send us a water bottle. It'll be no good tomorrow, God, as the baby will be dead, so please send it this afternoon."

While I gasped inwardly at the audacity of the prayer, she added by way of a corollary, "And while You are about it, would You please send a doll for the little girl so she'll know You really love her?"

As often with children's prayers, I was put on the spot. Could I honestly say, "Amen"? I just did not believe that God could do this. Oh, yes, I know that He can do everything. The Bible says so. But there are limits, aren't there? The only way God could answer this particular prayer would be by sending me a parcel from the home-land. I had been in Africa for almost four years at that time, and I had never, ever received a parcel from home. Anyway, if anyone did send me a parcel, who would put in a hot water bottle? I lived on the equator!

Halfway through the afternoon, while I was teach-ing in the nurses' training school, a message was sent that

*there was a car at my front door. By the time I reached
home, the car had gone, but there, on the verandah, was
a large twenty-two pound parcel. I felt tears pricking my
eyes. I could not open the parcel alone, so I sent for the
orphanage children. Together we pulled off the string,
carefully undoing each knot. We folded the paper, taking
care not to tear it unduly.*

*Excitement was mounting. Some thirty or forty pairs
of eyes were focused on the large cardboard box. From
the top, I lifted out brightly colored, knitted jerseys. Eyes
sparkled as I gave them out. Then there were the knitted bandages for the leprosy patients, and the children
looked a little bored. Then came a box of mixed raisins
and sultanas—that would make a nice batch of buns for
the weekend.*

*Then, as I put my hand in again, I felt. . .could it
really be? I grasped it and pulled it out. Yes, it was, a
brand-new, rubber hot water bottle!*

*I cried. I had not asked God to send it; I had not
truly believed that He could. Ruth was in the front row
of the children. She rushed forward, crying out, "If God
has sent the bottle, He must have sent the doll, too!"*

*Rummaging down to the bottom of the box, she pulled
out the small, beautifully dressed dolly. Her eyes shone! She
had never doubted. Looking up at me, she asked: "Can I
go over with you, Mummy, and give this doll to that little
girl, so she'll know that Jesus really loves her?"*

*That parcel had been on the way for five whole
months. Packed up by my former Sunday school class,
whose leader had heard and obeyed God's prompting
to send a hot water bottle, even to the equator. And one*

*of the girls had put in a doll for an African child—five
months before—in answer to the believing prayer of a
ten-year-old to bring it that afternoon! "Before they call,
I will answer!" (Isaiah 65:24).*[1]

## Making It Personal

I read stories like this and they remind me that God truly is
amazing. He can do miracles. He can do anything. Nothing is
too big, too hard, or too complicated for Him. He is the God
over all. He can send fire from heaven in answer to prayer. He
can deliver a hot-water bottle and doll to the Congo on exactly
the right day.

How big is God? Big enough! I could tell story after story
of how God worked in amazing ways as the result of desperate
prayer. But you don't need to hear someone else's story. You
need your own story.

What is your impossible situation? Where do you need a
miracle? Why not tell God? Ask Him to answer so you can give
Him the glory!

## NOTES

[1] Helen Roseveare, a missionary from England to Zaire, Africa, told this as
it had happened to her in Africa. She shared it in her testimony on
a Wednesday night at Thomas Road Baptist Church. It is also found
in her book, *Living Faith*, published by WEC International, P.O. Box
1707, Fort Washington, PA 19034. Used by permission.

# 10

# DELIVER US:

## *The Prayer of Hezekiah*

2 KINGS 19:19

Poor King Hezekiah faced a fate worse than his own death. The nightmare had the name Sennacherib, the undefeated king of Assyria. Sennacherib had a massive army and, in the literal sense, cutting-edge chariots. Sennacherib had already crushed all of the nations around Judah from Lebanon in the north to Egypt in the south. And now he was poised to ride his mighty war chariots right through Judah.

In order to intimidate Hezekiah, Sennacherib sent a message reminding Judah of his complete destruction of nine city-states that had opposed him. His message was clear. He intended to make Judah number ten unless they unconditionally put up a white flag and surrendered, then became slaves that were taken captive back to Assyria.

Hezekiah faced a deadly dilemma. Option A was to watch his nation get crushed by a superior force under the wheels of thundering chariots. Option B was to see his people shackled and led away to Assyria to be slaves. What could he do? What would you do?

Hezekiah chose Option C. He did what we all should do when we face extreme pressure and ferocious enemy attack. He prayed.

*Hezekiah received the letter from the messengers and read it. Then he went up to the temple of the LORD and spread it out before the LORD. And Hezekiah prayed to the LORD: "O LORD, God of Israel, enthroned between the cherubim, you alone are God over all the kingdoms of the earth. You have made heaven and earth. Give ear, O LORD, and hear; open your eyes, O LORD, and see; listen to the words Sennacherib has sent to insult the living God.*

*"It is true, O LORD, that the Assyrian kings have laid waste these nations and their lands. They have thrown their gods into the fire and destroyed them, for they were not gods but only wood and stone, fashioned by men's hands. Now, O LORD our God, deliver us from his hand, so that all kingdoms on earth may know that you alone, O LORD, are God."*

2 KINGS 19:14–19

## Deliver us.

Notice carefully the sentence "Now, O LORD our God, deliver us from his hand, so that all kingdoms on earth may know that you alone, O LORD, are God." This was the expression of Hezekiah's heart and the heart of his prayer. Hezekiah prayed a very simple prayer. The essence of it is captured in those two little words, "Deliver us." What else is there to say at times like that?

It turns out Option C was a great idea. Look at what happened.

*That night the angel of the LORD went out and put to death a hundred and eighty-five thousand men in the Assyrian camp. When the people got up the next morning—there were all the dead bodies!*

2 KINGS 19:35

Hezekiah was in a battle he had no shot at winning. Yet, God fought the battle for him. In the dark of night the angel of the Lord went out and killed such a massive number of the enemy that Sennacherib got God's message. Sennacherib was so shaken that he and his army packed up and marched straight home. They did not pass "Go" or collect $200.00. They didn't harass anyone else. They ran home like scared dogs.

God had not been impressed with the arrogance of Sennacherib, but God did like Hezekiah's prayer. Hezekiah's soldiers did not even have to fight! All Hezekiah's soldiers had to do was collect the booty that the Assyrians left in their haste. Hezekiah turned the problem over to God and God fought the battle and won.

Isn't it great serving a God who is both able and willing to deliver us when we ask? That is the promise of Psalm 91. Read it slowly.

> *He who dwells in the shelter of the Most High will rest in the shadow of the Almighty. I will say of the LORD, "He is my refuge and my fortress, my God, in whom I trust." Surely he will save you from the fowler's snare and from the deadly pestilence. He will cover you with his feathers, and under his wings you will find refuge; his faithfulness will be your shield and rampart. You will not fear the terror of night, nor the arrow that flies by day, nor the pestilence that stalks in the darkness, nor the plague that destroys at midday. A thousand may fall at your side, ten thousand at your right hand, but it will not come near you. You will only observe with your eyes and see the punishment of the wicked. If you make the Most High your dwelling—even the LORD, who is my refuge—then*

*no harm will befall you, no disaster will come near your
tent. For he will command his angels concerning you
to guard you in all your ways; they will lift you up in
their hands, so that you will not strike your foot against
a stone. You will tread upon the lion and the cobra; you
will trample the great lion and the serpent. "Because
he loves me," says the LORD, "I will rescue him; I will
protect him, for he acknowledges my name. He will call
upon me, and I will answer him; I will be with him in
trouble, I will deliver him and honor him. With long life
will I satisfy him and show him my salvation."*

What an awesome promise is this: "He will call upon me,
and I will answer him; I will be with him in trouble, I will
deliver him." In preparing this chapter, I came across many
modern-day stories of God's people calling out to Him and
God answering and delivering them. I don't have room to tell
them all, but let me summarize a few.

Nebio, a man who came to Christ in Ecuador, and two
missionary evangelists were caught in an ambush by angry vil-
lagers. Within minutes the attackers ran away. When Nebio
returned to the village, one man explained, "When they saw all
those soldiers on the ridge, they ran for their lives!"

Nebio used his experience to lead his entire family to the
Lord. Today there's a Christian church in that community with
many coming to Christ.[1]

Corrie Ten Boom told of an event during the Jeunesse
Rebellion in the Congo. An army of rebels approached a school
where children of missionaries lived. As the army of hundreds
advanced, the children and their teachers huddled in prayer.
Suddenly, the rebel force stopped and retreated. This happened

again the next day. Then the rebels left to fight elsewhere.

Later one of them was injured and was brought to the missionary school for treatment. The doctor asked him, "Why didn't you break into the school as you planned?"

"We couldn't do it," the soldier said, "When we saw the hundreds of soldiers in white uniforms, we became scared."[2]

Joan Wester Anderson records the story of Steve and Phil, two Christian plain-clothed police officers assigned to discover the source of the drugs ruining the community of Nutley, New Jersey. After prayer, they successfully found the hideout to be a cave. One night they chased a group of young adults to the cave. Praying Psalm 91, they found the cave held a dozen violent young adults, including their leader, Mr. Big, the drug dealer himself.

Unarmed but filled with courage, they went in and calmly apprehended Mr. Big and the rest. As they led their prisoners out, a police van pulled up to take them back to the station.

They asked Mr. Big, "Why didn't you or any of the others try to attack us when we came in?"

"You think I am crazy or something? There were at least twenty guys in blue uniforms."

"Twenty? No, there were just two of us," the officers replied.

"Hey, Belinda," Mr. Big called to another young prisoner, "how many cops came into the cave?"

Belinda shrugged, "At least twenty-five."[3]

In 2002 the Rodeo-Chediski forest fire consumed nearly half a million acres, roaring through much of Arizona. Firefighters labored valiantly to save the American Indian Christian Mission, but they were forced to leave when the blaze became too dangerous. Prayers from thousands of people were mingled with those of the children who asked God to deliver the mission.

It looked as though God had not heard their cries for

deliverance when the blaze roared up to within a few feet of the mission school on three sides. But God came through. Not one building was touched.

Interestingly, three crosses stood near the entrance to the school. In the inferno, only one was burned. It was the one in the middle. To those in the mission, that lone burned cross was a powerful reminder that Jesus Christ had saved the mission just as He has saved our souls, by being the one who is consumed.[4]

Myra worked for Teen Challenge in a very rough neighborhood in Philadelphia. A gang ruled the street outside the ministry center, harassing any young people who wanted to come to the center for help. One night when the gang appeared, Myra suddenly felt inspired to tell them about Jesus. She opened the door and walked outside. Instead of listening to her, the gang shouted threats of drowning her in the nearby river. Myra breathed a prayer to Jesus. "Lord, let your angels come with me and protect me," she murmured.

Then she opened the door and was about to speak when the gang members suddenly stopped their shouting, turned to look at one another, and left silently and quickly. Myra was surprised. Why had they gone?

The gang did not return for several days. Then one afternoon, to the surprise of everyone, they entered the center in an orderly fashion. Much later, after a relationship had been built with them, they were asked what had made them leave so peacefully that night.

One young man said, "We wouldn't dare touch her after her boyfriend showed up. That dude had to be seven feet tall."

"I didn't know Myra had a boyfriend," they were told. "But at any rate, she was here alone that night."

"No, we saw him," insisted another gang member. "He was right behind her. He was big as life in his classy white suit."[5]

## Making It Personal

Asking God for deliverance from evil is definitely a prayer God delights to answer. We don't have to be facing urgent danger to use it. You may recall that when Jesus gave us the sample prayer, He taught us to regularly pray, "Deliver us from evil or from the evil one" (Matthew 6:13).

Only God knows what evil awaits you today. You don't need to face it alone. God fights many battles for us, especially when we ask Him to deliver us. Make "Deliver us" one of your daily prayers. When you get to heaven, you will be able to see "behind the veil" of how many times God answered, even times when you did not ask for His help.

## NOTES

[1] Dr. Ron Cline, "Protecting Angels," a message given at HCJB World Radio, Tuesday, May 18, 2004.

[2] Corrie Ten Boom, *Marching Orders for the End Battle* (Fort Washington, PA: Christian Literature Crusade, 1969), pp. 89–90.

[3] Joan Wester Anderson, *Where Angels Walk* (New York, NY: Ballantine Books, 1992), pp. 216–18.

[4] Rachel Clark, "Arizona Fire Leaves Long Term Burden," *Disaster News Network* (www.disasternews.net), September 2002.

[5] Betty Malz, *Angels Watching Over Me* (Old Tappan, NJ: Chosen Books, 1986), pp. 97–98.

# 11

# HELP US:

## *The Prayer of Asa*

### 2 CHRONICLES 14:11

If you haven't been there yet, you will be. Mark it down. There will be those times when there is nothing else you can do. There is nowhere else to turn. You need big-time help and you need it now. You need God.

Maybe you read that first paragraph and nodded your head. When despair, helplessness, and hopelessness are mentioned, they resonate deep within. You understand what it means to be swept up in that current and somehow live to tell about it. You know exactly what I am writing about. You have been there and done that. And guess what? Times like that will probably happen again.

Maybe you don't think such crises will ever happen to you. Just ask Asa.

All was going great for Asa. He was the golden boy. As the king of Judah, he seemed to be doing everything right. During his first ten years in office, he radically cleaned up and significantly built up the nation.

*And Abijah rested with his fathers and was buried in the City of David. Asa his son succeeded him as king, and in his days the country was at peace for ten years. Asa*

*did what was good and right in the eyes of the LORD his*
*God. He removed the foreign altars and the high places,*
*smashed the sacred stones and cut down the Asherah*
*poles. He commanded Judah to seek the LORD, the God*
*of their fathers, and to obey his laws and commands. He*
*removed the high places and incense altars in every town*
*in Judah, and the kingdom was at peace under him. He*
*built up the fortified cities of Judah, since the land was at*
*peace. No one was at war with him during those years,*
*for the LORD gave him rest. "Let us build up these towns,"*
*he said to Judah, "and put walls around them, with tow-*
*ers, gates and bars. The land is still ours, because we have*
*sought the LORD our God; we sought him and he has*
*given us rest on every side." So they built and prospered.*
*Asa had an army of three hundred thousand men from*
*Judah, equipped with large shields and with spears, and*
*two hundred and eighty thousand from Benjamin, armed*
*with small shields and with bows. All these were brave*
*fighting men.*

2 CHRONICLES 14:1–8

That was a highly impressive decade as Asa did what was right in the eyes of God. He tore down the tools of pagan worship. He led his people to seek God and obey His commands. He strengthened the fortified cities and assembled a large, well-equipped army. He had every reason to assume his good fortune would continue and peace would perpetuate.

He was woefully wrong.

*Zerah the Cushite marched out against them with a vast*
*army and three hundred chariots, and came as far as*

> *Mareshah. Asa went out to meet him, and they took up*
> *battle positions in the Valley of Zephathah near Mareshah.*
>
> 2 CHRONICLES 14:9–10

All was sweet and joyful in Judah until one decisive day when a dark cloud rolled up from Egypt. In the eye of the terrible tempest was Zerah, leading a massive war machine of one million Ethiopians and three hundred gleaming chariots. Asa would have to face a skilled opponent who had him outnumbered by over four hundred thousand troops, which was bad enough. But what made it worse were those three hundred war wagons. Judah had no defense against the awesome speed and power of the best modern weapons of mass destruction on the planet in 900 BC. It would be one of the most massive massacres in history.

How would you handle the horrible hopelessness of facing definite defeat and destruction? What do you usually do when things are bleak?

Asa did the right thing. He prayed one of the most effective prayers recorded in the Bible.

> *Then Asa called to the LORD his God and said, "LORD,*
> *there is no one like you to help the powerless against the*
> *mighty. Help us, O LORD our God, for we rely on you, and*
> *in your name we have come against this vast army. O LORD,*
> *you are our God; do not let man prevail against you."*
>
> 1 CHRONICLES 14:11

**Help us, O Lord our God.**
What an excellent pattern for effective prayer! The prayer is short—only twenty-seven words in Hebrew—and complete. Moreover, Asa's simple petition consists of three outstanding components of effective prayer:

1. *He opened with appropriate words of praise:* "Lord, there is no one like you to help the powerless against the mighty." Praise positions us to pray.

2. *He stated the petition clearly and succinctly:* "Help us, O LORD our God."

3. *He gave God the reasons he expected Him to answer—in his case, four reasons.* First, Judah was depending on God, not on themselves or anyone else: "for we rely on you." Second, Judah was representing God in this cause: "in your name we have come against this vast army." Third, Israel belonged to and was allied with God: "O LORD, you are our God." Fourth, ultimately the battle was the Lord's: "do not let man prevail against you."

It worked, and then some. God heard Asa's prayer and gave him a miraculous answer, exceedingly and abundantly above all he asked or thought.

> The LORD struck down the Cushites before Asa and Judah. The Cushites fled, and Asa and his army pursued them as far as Gerar. Such a great number of Cushites fell that they could not recover; they were crushed before the LORD and his forces. The men of Judah carried off a large amount of plunder. They destroyed all the villages around Gerar, for the terror of the LORD had fallen upon them. They plundered all these villages, since there was much booty there. They also attacked the camps of the herdsmen and carried off droves of sheep and goats and camels. Then they returned to Jerusalem.
>
> 1 CHRONICLES 14:12–15

God sent such a holy terror upon the Cushites that they ran away in fear before the battle began. Exactly how God did it, the Bible does not say. That'll be something we find out in heaven when we watch the movie in the "You Were There Theater." Maybe He sent a host of glimmering angels who blinded them in the early morning sunrise. Maybe He spoke in a thunderous voice. Maybe He painted a million different images of their secret nightmares across the canvas of their minds. It will be fun to find out.

They were too scared to fight and were routed by Judah's army. All Asa and his men had to do was chase them. Amazingly, the huge Ethiopian force had been completely conquered by Asa's smaller army.

Yet, God not only gave them a victory, but He gave them prodigious plunder. Judah grabbed up what the fleeing Cushites left behind as well as pillaged the Philistine villages that made the costly error of housing those Cushites. On top of that, Judah was able to defeat and fleece the rich camps of the pesty nomadic herdsmen who had been following the Cushite army selling them sheep, goats, and camels.

Can you imagine how excited and happy everyone was when the victorious troops marched back into Jerusalem with the precious prizes and bountiful booty? Not only were they spared probable annihilation and certain slavery, they were free. The margin of victory was not even close. They totally crushed the opponent.

Asa's prayer was more than effective. It was miraculously, powerfully, liberatingly, wealth-producingly potent.

Help us, O Lord our God.

## Making It Personal

1. *You can tap into the overlooked power of God by crying out for help.* Consider the story of the prophet Jonah, who was running

from God. When he was thrown from a ship in the midst of a terrible storm, he had two choices: drown or pray. He prayed and asked God for help: "In my distress I called to the LORD, and he answered me. From the depths of the grave I called for help, and you listened to my cry" (Jonah 2:2).

God sent a great fish to swallow Jonah. The fish saved Jonah's life and delivered him to where he was supposed to have gone in the first place, the evil city of Nineveh.

> From inside the fish, Jonah prayed to the LORD his God. He said: "In my distress I called to the LORD, and he answered me. From the depths of the grave I called for help, and you listened to my cry. . . ." And the LORD commanded the fish, and it vomited Jonah onto dry land.
>
> JONAH 2:1, 10

Riding through the sea inside a fish couldn't have been the most luxurious mode of travel, and being vomited out is not the most fashionable way to make an entrance. But for a man who should have been dead it wasn't bad. Tap into the power of God and be saved!

2. *Praying Asa's prayer may result in an answer exceedingly and abundantly above all you could ask or think.* Think of Daniel the prophet, who spent most of his life as an exile in Babylon. When Daniel discovered that his commitment to God would lead to being thrown into the lions' den, he asked God for help: "Then these men went as a group and found Daniel praying and asking God for help" (Daniel 6:11).

God answered Daniel's prayer for help and gave Daniel multi-layered blessings as a result. First, though, Daniel was miraculously protected from the lions. He told the king, "My

God sent his angel, and he shut the mouths of the lions. They have not hurt me, because I was found innocent in his sight" (Daniel 6:22). Beyond that, Daniel's enemies were removed and the pagan king Darius glorified the Lord by telling Daniel's testimony to the nation.

> *"May you prosper greatly! I issue a decree that in every part of my kingdom people must fear and reverence the God of Daniel. For he is the living God and he endures forever; his kingdom will not be destroyed, his dominion will never end. He rescues and he saves; he performs signs and wonders in the heavens and on the earth. He has rescued Daniel from the power of the lions."*
> *So Daniel prospered during the reign of Darius.*
> DANIEL 6:25–28

3. *If you need help today, God is listening.* The Psalms are full of examples of survival prayer. Notice the word "help" in each of these passages.

> *God is our refuge and strength, an ever-present help in trouble. Therefore we will not fear, though the earth give way and the mountains fall into the heart of the sea.*
> PSALM 46:1–2

> *I lift up my eyes to the hills—where does my help come from? My help comes from the LORD, the Maker of heaven and earth.*
> PSALM 121:1–2

> *Come quickly to help me, O Lord my Savior.*
> PSALM 38:22

*Be pleased, O LORD, to save me; O LORD, come quickly to help me.*

PSALM 40:13

*Then my enemies will turn back when I call for help. By this I will know that God is for me.*

PSALM 56:9

*Hasten, O God, to save me; O LORD, come quickly to help me.*

PSALM 70:1

*Yet I am poor and needy; come quickly to me, O God. You are my help and my deliverer; O LORD, do not delay.*

PSALM 70:5

*Help us, O God our Savior, for the glory of your name; deliver us and forgive our sins for your name's sake.*

PSALM 79:9

*Our help is in the name of the LORD, the Maker of heaven and earth.*

PSALM 124:8

Do you need help today? Ask God. He's listening, He's able, and He's willing.

# 12

# GRANT ME FAVOR:
## *The Prayer of Nehemiah*
### NEHEMIAH 1:11

Maybe you know exactly what you need to happen and where you need God to work. Yet, God first might work through someone in authority over you. That person could be a government official, teacher, or pastor or maybe even your boss, coach, parent, or spouse! But in order to get what you need, God has to move their hearts on your behalf.

As the cupbearer for King Artaxerxes, Nehemiah held a very responsible position, yet he longed to be eight hundred miles away, back with his people in the destroyed city of Jerusalem. They were facing possible annihilation and Nehemiah needed to return to rebuild the city walls. More specifically, he needed three years off from his job and enough supplies to rebuild a wall around the entire city of Jerusalem! First, though, a huge change had to happen in the heart of the man in authority, that is, King Artaxerxes. Nehemiah's superior, an unbeliever, had a nasty reputation for cutting the heads off subordinates who upset him. For Nehemiah to march into the king's oval office and demand time off and building materials would be signing his own death warrant. So what could he do?

If you read the story of Nehemiah, you find a man who

consistently turned his problems into prayer. He lived by the advice, "Pray when troubles trouble you." We find him turning his problems into prayer in almost every one of the twelve chapters in the book bearing his name (Nehemiah 1:5–11; 2:5; 4:4–5, 9; 5:19; 6:9–14; 9:32; 13:14, 22, 29, 31). So when the need in Jerusalem was brought to his attention, he did as he always did. He brought the matter to the Lord. His prayer, one of the most effective in the Bible, is a tutorial on how to pray. Let's see what we can learn from him.

Nehemiah opened with words of praise and perspective. God's address is praise. Praise and thanksgiving are gateways into the presence of God (see Psalm 100:4). He also mentions the perspective that the God he is addressing is the one who keeps His covenant. The importance of this will become clear as the prayer develops.

> *Then I said: "O LORD, God of heaven, the great and awesome God, who keeps his covenant of love with those who love him and obey his commands."*
>
> NEHEMIAH 1:5

Nehemiah did not pray once and quit. He brought his burden to God repeatedly, day and night. It may have been weeks or even months from when he first began to pray about the plight of Jerusalem until God granted his request.

Jesus made a promise when He said, "keep on asking and it shall be given unto you" (a literal translation of Matthew 7:7). He also encouraged us to be as persistent in our prayers as the friend at midnight (Luke 11:5–10) and the widow who beseeched the unjust judge (Luke 18:1–8).

*"Let your ear be attentive and your eyes open to hear the prayer your servant is praying before you day and night for your servants, the people of Israel."*

NEHEMIAH 1:6

Nehemiah then moved to a season of assessment and confession of sins. Because sin creates a barrier between God and us (Isaiah 59:1–2), it removes God's obligation to hear and answer prayer (Psalm 66:18). So Nehemiah confessed his sins.

*"I confess the sins we Israelites, including myself and my father's house, have committed against you. We have acted very wickedly toward you. We have not obeyed the commands, decrees and laws you gave your servant Moses."*

NEHEMIAH 1:6–7

Note that Nehemiah confesses not only his own sins but also those of his people. The big request he is going to make is not all about Nehemiah. Should God say "Yes" to Nehemiah's petition, the answer will bless all of God's people.

Nehemiah reminded God of the promise He made through Moses. God had promised that the people would be scattered through disobedience and they were. He also promised that they would be returned through obedience. This was the key to Nehemiah's expectation: that God would act on his behalf, and that God had a soft spot for His people in whom He had already invested so much.

*"Remember the instruction you gave your servant Moses, saying, 'If you are unfaithful, I will scatter you among the nations, but if you return to me and obey my commands,*

*then even if your exiled people are at the farthest hori-*
*zon, I will gather them from there and bring them to the*
*place I have chosen as a dwelling for my Name.' They are*
*your servants and your people, whom you redeemed by*
*your great strength and your mighty hand."*

NEHEMIAH 1:8–10

Those skilled in the art of intercession apply the importance of the timely use of God's promises. There are hundreds of promises in the Bible, one for every need. Claiming them in prayer and reminding God of His promises gives us boldness in prayer.

When the Israelites escaped Egypt and wandered in the wilderness, they rebelled against God. God told Moses that He would destroy them (Exodus 32:7–10). Yet, Moses pleaded the promises God had made to Abraham, Isaac, and Israel (Exodus 32:11–13). Moses' appeal worked! God relented and spared the entire nation (Exodus 32:14; Psalm 106:23).

Nehemiah got down to business and offered his petition:

*"O Lord, let your ear be attentive to the prayer of this*
*your servant and to the prayer of your servants who*
*delight in revering your name. Give your servant success*
*today by granting him favor in the presence of this man."*
*I was cupbearer to the king.*

NEHEMIAH 1:11

### Grant favor.

Nehemiah must have been familiar with the book of Genesis and with the prayer of Abraham's servant, "Give me success today." But he did not stop there. He told God specifically how he needed success: "Give your servant success today by *granting him favor* in the presence of this man." "This man" was none other than Nehemiah's boss, the most powerful man on the planet, King Artaxerxes. Nehemiah's petition was that God would touch the king's heart in such a way as to give favor to Nehemiah and give him what he needed. Nehemiah was going to ask the king to send him off with his blessing to rebuild the walls *and* for the resources to pay for it!

The nature, size, and scope of Nehemiah's request were such that the odds of Artaxerxes saying "Yes" were slim. That's why Nehemiah went to God first. God would have to touch the king's heart before he would ever agree to Nehemiah's petition.

And He did, but not without a little nail biting. See for yourself:

> *In the month of Nisan in the twentieth year of King Artaxerxes, when wine was brought for him, I took the wine and gave it to the king. I had not been sad in his presence before; so the king asked me, "Why does your face look so sad when you are not ill? This can be nothing but sadness of heart." I was very much afraid.*
>
> NEHEMIAH 2:1–2

Of course he was afraid! It was a capital offense to appear in the king's presence with an unhappy face. He was hoping that his prayer would hold up. What else could he do?

Nehemiah acted on the belief that God would answer. There is a time for prayer and there is a time for action. Now was the time to act.

> *But I said to the king, "May the king live forever! Why should my face not look sad when the city where my fathers*

*are buried lies in ruins, and its gates have been destroyed by fire?" The king said to me, "What is it you want?"*

NEHEMIAH 2:3–4

This was the big moment. If Nehemiah did not have the king's favor, asking for such an outlandish thing would be fatal. If he did have the king's favor for such a huge request, it would be a miracle. God had to come through. So he reminded God of his request.

Nehemiah kept praying until the answer arrived.

*Then I prayed to the God of heaven, and I answered the king, "If it pleases the king and if your servant has found favor in his sight, let him send me to the city in Judah where my fathers are buried so that I can rebuild it."*

NEHEMIAH 2:4–5

Gulp. Nehemiah's fate, the fate of Jerusalem, and the fate of the Israelites rested on the response of the king.

*Then the king, with the queen sitting beside him, asked me, "How long will your journey take, and when will you get back?" It pleased the king to send me; so I set a time.*

NEHEMIAH 2:6

Did you see it? He said, "It pleased the king to send me." Unbelievable, impossible, amazing! God came through. Nehemiah was on a roll. Instead of quitting while he was ahead, he pressed on.

Nehemiah did not give up until he received all he needed.

*I also said to him, "If it pleases the king, may I have let-*
*ters to the governors of Trans-Euphrates, so that they will*
*provide me safe-conduct until I arrive in Judah? And*
*may I have a letter to Asaph, keeper of the king's forest,*
*so he will give me timber to make beams for the gates of*
*the citadel by the temple and for the city wall and for the*
*residence I will occupy?"*

NEHEMIAH 2:7–8

First, God worked so the king would let him go. Now, Nehemiah was asking the king to pay for safe conduct and supplies. Did he go too far?

*And because the gracious hand of my God was upon me,*
*the king granted my requests. So I went to the governors*
*of Trans-Euphrates and gave them the king's letters. The*
*king had also sent army officers and cavalry with me.*

NEHEMIAH 2:8–9

The king gave Nehemiah all he asked for plus an army escort! Coincidence? No way. Nehemiah knew why the king showed him such incredible favor. He said it was because the gracious hand of his God was upon him.

Gaining the favor of Artaxerxes was a big obstacle to Nehemiah, but the power of Nehemiah's God dwarfed it. The king's heart was putty in God's hands. Nehemiah received exceedingly and abundantly more than he had asked or thought.

## Making It Personal

God *is* able to change the hearts of those in authority. A friend who serves as an associate pastor recently told me how discouraged he had been by the refusal of his church's leadership to allow him to make necessary changes in the way the church did ministry. After the friend patiently prayed for favor, God touched their hearts and the changes are taking place. On top of that, he received a promotion and a raise!

God is able to change hearts, and I have seen that most recently in my own life. After weeks of prayer, God granted my son favor with his school's superintendent concerning a very challenging and difficult decision. God's favor cleared the way for a positive response toward my son.

Who needs to grant you favor if you are to carry out your ministry? With whom do you need favor if you are going to be able to follow God's heart? "Grant me favor" is one prayer we may need to use often. Start praying it now, and see what God can do for you.

# 13

## STRENGTHEN MY HANDS:
### The Prayer of Nehemiah
#### NEHEMIAH 6:9

Weary and tottering on the brink of despair, Nehemiah had been working for brutally long days week after week. He was attempting the impossible. His task was to lead a remnant of God's people in the impossible task of rebuilding the walls of Jerusalem.

All during the weeks of work, a strong enemy named Sanballat and his friends had attempted to discourage Nehemiah and his workers by laughing at their vision (Nehemiah 2:19) and later criticizing and belittling their efforts (4:1–3). When that failed, they gathered a coalition force to frighten and intimidate the workers with the threat of a surprise attack (4:7–12). On top of that, there was division in the ranks of Nehemiah's workforce (5:1–13). Yet, through it all, Nehemiah's integrity, courage, and God-focused encouragement kept the work moving ahead until the walls were nearly completed.

At that point, Nehemiah desperately needed some relief and rest. Instead, things got worse. Before he could catch his breath, his cunning nemesis Sanballat tried a new approach. Repeatedly, he requested meetings with Nehemiah. Yet, Nehemiah wisely refused each request, sensing that Sanballat wanted, at the very least, to distract him from the task. Most probably, Sanballat wanted to lure Nehemiah away so he could kidnap or kill him.

After four refusals, Sanballat launched a devious new scheme. He cleverly misrepresented Nehemiah's motives, character, and methods in an open letter. In it, Sanballat even stated that Nehemiah was rebuilding the wall to make himself rich and powerful. These unsubstantiated and inaccurate rumors were designed to undercut Nehemiah's authority (see Nehemiah 6:5–7).

Oh, the ruinous nature of rumors! They pierce deeply, as did Sanballat's carefully crafted lies about Nehemiah. Yet, Nehemiah would not quit.

Note that God does not make it easy on His people. Just because we are trying to do as God wants does not mean that we will be immune to problems, frustrations, and attacks. Just the opposite is true.

Yet, Nehemiah fought on by fighting from his knees. He turned his problems into prayer. This was not a new thing for Nehemiah. Prayer was part of his lifestyle. Looking over the book that bears his name reveals his relentless reliance on prayer. First, Nehemiah turned his burden for the broken-down walls into prayer (Nehemiah 1:5–11). Then he turned the potential disaster of his appointment with the king into prayer (2:4). As he began building the walls, he prayed his way out of Sanballat's early assaults (4:4–5). Now as he faced back-breaking weariness and undeserved attack, Nehemiah turned again to prayer:

> *They were all trying to frighten us, thinking, "Their hands will get too weak for the work, and it will not be completed." But I prayed, "Now strengthen my hands."*
>
> NEHEMIAH 6:9

### Strengthen my hands.

Nehemiah did not ask God to wipe out his enemies, as I might have done. He did not ask God to give this daunting responsibility to someone else, which I almost surely would have. He did not even ask for the walls to be miraculously built by legions of angels overnight, which I would at least have tried. Instead, he prayed, "Strengthen my hands."

Sometimes God prefers to do the miracle *in* us.

"Strengthen my hands." And God responded, as is revealed in the first five words of verse 15: "So the wall was completed on the twenty-fifth of Elul, in fifty-two days" (Nehemiah 6:15).

The wall was completed in a mere fifty-two days. No one would have believed it possible. Engineers are still marveling at the accomplishment. Mission Impossible became Mission Accomplished!

And make no mistake: This material structure was the result of spiritual activity. Prayer guided, fueled, forced, and completed the impossible. Nehemiah refused to quit, and God did not fail to bless. Yet, that's not all. When God gave Nehemiah strength to complete the project, his enemies became so discouraged that they were led to acknowledge that the rebuilding of the walls was the work of God!

> *When all our enemies heard about this, all the surrounding nations were afraid and lost their self-confidence, because they realized that this work had been done with the help of our God.*
>
> NEHEMIAH 6:16

Charles Swindoll has written, "That has to be the most thrilling experience in the world—to watch God come to the rescue when you have been helpless. In the middle of the incessant assault of the enemy, in spite of endless verbal barrage, the wall was built! While the enemy blasts, God builds."[1]

## Making It Personal

1. *Nehemiah was not the first to find God as his source of strength.* From the Psalms we read:

> *The LORD is the strength of his people, a fortress of salvation for his anointed one.*
>
> PSALM 28:8

> *God is our refuge and strength, an ever-present help in trouble.*
>
> PSALM 46:1

> *My flesh and my heart may fail, but God is the strength of my heart and my portion forever.*
>
> PSALM 73:26

> *Sing for joy to God our strength; shout aloud to the God of Jacob!*
>
> PSALM 81:1

2. *Nehemiah also was not the only one to ask God for strength.* The Psalmist prayed, "My soul is weary with sorrow; strengthen me according to your word" (Psalm 119:28). The prophet Isaiah prayed, "O LORD, be gracious to us; we long for you. Be our strength every morning, our salvation in time of distress" (Isaiah 33:2).

Samson, the world's strongest man, forfeited his strength when he lost his connection to God, courtesy of his fateful haircut in Delilah's beauty salon (Judges 16:4–21), which then led to his blinding and imprisonment. You might not recall the rest of the story. The Philistines were having a party in honor of their god, Dagon, and they brought Samson out to entertain the guests. After he was finished, they chained him between the pillars of the great temple to Dagon. Then Samson did something he should have been doing all along (Judges 16:23–27):

> *Then Samson prayed to the LORD, "O Sovereign LORD, remember me. O God, please strengthen me just once more, and let me with one blow get revenge on the Philistines for my two eyes."*

> JUDGES 16:28

Sadly, Samson's death was his greatest triumph. He had finally learned the frailty of human strength and the necessity of divine power. He prayed, "Strengthen me." And God did.

"Strengthen me." I find this prayer to be one I use often. Life will wear us out and responsibility will wear us down. The added pressure of the attacks of an "enemy" rapidly erodes our strength.

Many pastors are a little like Nehemiah when it comes to building projects. I have helped lead our church through four major building projects, and every one was riddled with its own unique challenges, opponents, and frustrations. I have learned to ask God to strengthen my hands, and He has come through on every occasion.

3. *God can give you enough strength today for whatever challenge you are facing.* The greater the obstacles, the greater His strength. One man found this out in a miraculous fashion.

Stanley got up early on September 11, 2001, and left for work in the World Trade Center Tower Two where he was the assistant vice-president of loans for a bank. That morning in his quiet time with God, Stanley felt an unusual need to ask God for strength and protection.

Later, as he sat in his office talking on the phone, he looked up to see what he would later know was United Airlines Flight 175 heading straight toward him. "All I can see is this big gray plane, with red letters on the wing and on the tail, bearing down on me." It seemed like it was happening in slow motion. All he could do was pray, "Lord, you take control, I can't help myself here."

Just before the plane hit, Stanley dove under his desk. Immediately the plane tore into the side of the building and exploded. Flaming rubble filled the room.

Somehow, Stanley was unhurt. But from under the desk he could see the flaming wing of the plane blocking his doorway. He knew he had to get out of his office, but how? He was trapped in debris as high as his shoulders.

"Lord, you take control, this is your problem now," he prayed. Later he said, the Lord "gave me so much power and strength in my body that I was able to shake everything off. I felt like the strongest man alive."

Stanley's office resembled a war zone, with walls flattened into dusty heaps, office furniture strewn violently around, flames dancing menacingly, and heavy rubble everywhere. He would somehow have to get through it all to escape.

"Everything I'm trying to climb on [to get out] is collapsing," he recalled. "I was getting cuts and bruises, but I'm saying, 'Lord I have to go home to my loved ones, I have to make it. You have to help me.' " In other words, "Give me strength."

His heart sank when he came to a wall. He could not go back into the flames and he could not go on through the wall. Again, he prayed for strength. "I got up, and I felt as if a power came over me," he said. "I felt goose bumps all over my body and I'm trembling, and I said to the wall, " 'You're going to be no match for me and my Lord.' " Then he punched through the wall.

On the other side was a man named Brian who desperately needed help. To get out alive they had to somehow get down eighty-one flights of rubble-filled steps trapped in the heart of a burning building. Praying for strength, they descended step after step, flight by flight. Finally, they reached the concourse. The only people there were firefighters.

The weary men now faced a wall of flames. They soaked themselves in the building sprinkler system to run through the flames. Praying all the way, they burst through the flames, out of the building, and to the safety of a church two blocks away. "As soon as I held onto the gate of that church, the building [World Trade Center Tower Two] collapsed," Stanley recalled.

Hours later, cut and bloody, with clothes tattered and wearing a borrowed shirt, Stanley Praimnath made it home to his wife, Jennifer, and his two girls, Stephanie, 8, and Caitlin, 4. "I held my wife and my two children and we cried," Stanley said. Then they thanked God.[2]

If God can give Nehemiah, Samson, and Stanley strength, He certainly can give you the strength you need. Ask Him.

## NOTES

[1]Charles Swindoll, *Hand Me Another Brick* (Nashville, TN: Thomas Nelson, 1978), p. 137.

[2]Adapted from Dan Van Veen, "Surviving the 81st Floor of World Trade Tower Two," Assemblies of God News Service, September 14, 2001. Copyright © 2002 The General Council of the Assemblies of God, 1445 North Boonville Ave., Springfield, MO 65802. Used by permission of Stanley Praimnath.

# 14

# SEND ME:

## Isaiah's Response to God's Call

ISAIAH 6:8

What do you usually say when God comes calling? What should you say?

The way you answer can change your life. . .and the lives of many others. Let me explain, using the life of an Israelite named Isaiah.

In 739 BC, Isaiah was a restless young man in a seething nation. The last good king had died, leaving the Israelites hanging in the balance between prosperity and destruction. As a righteous and sensitive young man, Isaiah felt his country's pain and ached to do something about it. As a God seeker, he longed for a more intimate relationship with God. And God obliged both passions. Let's read how it happened.

> *In the year that King Uzziah died, I saw the Lord seated on a throne, high and exalted, and the train of his robe filled the temple. Above him were seraphs, each with six wings: With two wings they covered their faces, with two they covered their feet, and with two they were flying. And they were calling to one another: "Holy, holy, holy is the LORD Almighty; the whole earth is full of his glory." At*

*the sound of their voices the doorposts and thresholds shook
and the temple was filled with smoke. "Woe to me!" I
cried. "I am ruined! For I am a man of unclean lips, and
I live among a people of unclean lips, and my eyes have
seen the King, the LORD Almighty." Then one of the seraphs flew to me with a live coal in his hand, which he had
taken with tongs from the altar. With it he touched my
mouth and said, "See, this has touched your lips; your guilt
is taken away and your sin atoned for." Then I heard the
voice of the Lord saying, "Whom shall I send? And who
will go for us?" And I said, "Here am I. Send me!"*

ISAIAH 6:1–8

Isaiah was one of the few persons still living on earth that was
privileged to peer into heaven. Can you imagine seeing the Lord?
Isaiah's vision of the throne room put God in perspective. He is
vastly unlike all others. God is majestic, seated on a throne. He is
supreme, high, and exalted. But above all, He is holy, very holy.

We know God is holy because He is the only being in the
universe worshiped by seraphs. The Hebrew word *seraph* means
"burning." We may hope that God is a big, soft, teddy bear, but
the Bible tells us that God is a consuming fire (Hebrews 12:29).
Seraphs are unique angels who fly constantly around the throne
of God. These asbestos-like wonders experience spontaneous
and eternal combustion without consumption because they are
so near to God.

God's holiness is made clear from the antiphonal calls of the
seraphs. They perpetually cry out, "Holy, holy, holy is the LORD
Almighty; the whole earth is full of His glory." God has many
attributes, but those closest to Him recognize that His dominant
one is His surpassing holiness. It is so overpoweringly pervasive

that all the seraphs can do is repeat over and over to each other, "Holy, holy, holy," in an eternal symphony to Him.

Thirdly, Isaiah's response to God signifies His incredible holiness. When Isaiah saw God up close and personal, he did not sit down and chat, or stand up and cheer, or kick back and relax. He fell down and repented. "Woe is me," he cried. "I am ruined." A literal translation might read, "I am condemned guilty of sin and am melting away in the oven-blast brilliancy of God's holiness."

In His mercy God did not leave Isaiah in the misery of condemnation. Instead, He saw that Isaiah was cleansed. Yet, what is especially striking to me is that God not only cleansed Isaiah, but He called him. Both Isaiah and God were keenly aware of Israel's need for a new prophet. In Isaiah, God had found one. Humble and clean vessels are what God is seeking to pour Himself through. When Isaiah became clean, God called, "Whom shall I send? And who will go for us?"

This call resonated deep within Isaiah. It must have been tied to something God had written on Isaiah's heart before he was born. Maybe Isaiah had been aware of it before, or maybe this was the first moment of recognition. Either way, Isaiah did not hesitate to respond. He could not wait, so he said, "Here am I. Send me!"

### Send me.

"Send me." This effective prayer caused God to respond by sending Isaiah to his own people to deliver message after message of necessary and convicting warning. And God also sent Isaiah to us, as he would record his messages in what would become sixty-six chapters in the book bearing his name.

Isaiah is one of the most amazing books ever written. The promises found in it, especially in chapters 40 and later, are some of my favorites. Yet, beyond the promises are the incredible prophecies. There are prophecies about Israel and her neighboring nations that came true during Isaiah's own lifetime, as well as dozens of predictions about the Messiah seven hundred years before Jesus was born. They all came true with outlandish accuracy. Beyond that, his many eschatological prophecies give us great insight into the end times and the coming kingdom of God.

"Send me" is one prayer God delights to answer. I know from experience.

*I woke up that day just like every other day. I read a few chapters of my Bible and briefly prayed about the day. The only thing out of the ordinary was that I did something I had only done on a few other occasions. I happened to specifically pray a "send me" prayer. I told God to send me to make a difference in someone's life for His sake. Then I forgot about it and went off to work.*

*All morning long I had a gnawing thought.* I need a haircut. I ought to go to the mall and get it. *I am a thrifty (some might even say cheap) person. I had never gone to the salon in the mall for a haircut before. I usually saved money by having some student on campus do it for a few bucks. But over and over I kept getting the thought that I needed to go to the mall for a haircut.*

*Just before lunch I remembered that I had prayed the "send me" prayer that morning. It hit me like a thunderbolt. "It must be God!" I realized. "But why is He sending me to the mall? What could He want me to do for Him by getting a haircut?"*

*Yet when the thought immediately returned, I got up,*

*grabbed my coat, and headed for my car. I must confess
that I was grumbling as I drove the short distance to
the mall.* I wonder how much this haircut is going to
cost? How will I explain to Cathy my sudden urge for
extravagance? Why would God want me to go to the
mall? Why couldn't God give me a more glamorous
assignment?

*I walked into the hair salon and was given the only
open chair. A young woman put a sheet around my
neck and asked me how I wanted my hair cut. Then we
engaged in small talk. As we did, she asked me where I
worked. I told her that I was the campus pastor of the
Christian university down the road.*

*"Oh my God!" she gasped. (I became worried at
this point because she was holding scissors and I was
unarmed.) "I don't believe this!" she said as she started to
cry. "This morning as I got ready for work, I told God
I would give Him one last chance. If He did not send
me a Christian to talk to today, I was going to end it all
tonight."*

*Now I understood why I was sent to the mall to get
a haircut. As a result of our conversation, she got her life
back on track with God. And I gained a deeper apprecia-
tion for the power of "send me" prayers.*[1]

When Christian author Henry Blackaby pastored Faith Baptist Church in Saskatoon, Saskatchewan, he began to sense God
leading the congregation to an outreach ministry on the college
campus. Neither he nor the church had worked with students,
and furthermore, for two years the church had tried to start a
Bible study in the dorms without success. One Sunday they

decided to ask God what His will was for the congregation and to use them. Read how God responded:

> *On Wednesday one of the girls reported, "Oh, Pastor, a girl who had been in class with me for two years came to me after class today. She said, 'I think you might be a Christian. I need to talk to you.' I remembered what you had said. I had a class, but I missed it. We went to the cafeteria to talk. She said, 'Eleven of us girls in the dorm have been studying the Bible, and none of us are Christians. Do you know someone who can lead us in a Bible study?'" As a result of that contact we started three Bible studies in the women's dorms and two in the men's dorm. Over the following years many of those students trusted Christ as Savior and Lord. Many of those surrendered to full-time ministry and are now serving as pastors and missionaries all over the world.*[2]

After telling this story, Blackaby gave a wise word of caution and encouragement.

> *When the love relationship [with God] is right, He is free to give you assignments at His initiative. Whenever you do not seem to be receiving assignments from God, focus on the love relationship and stay there until the assignment comes.*[3]

Bruce Wilkinson tells of God's quick and specific response to his wife's request to be used of God. "A neighbor we hardly knew came knocking on our door. 'Ma'am,' she said through tears. 'My husband is dying, and I have no one to talk to. Can you help me?' "[4]

In speaking about the adventure of asking God to use us, Wilkinson writes,

"People will show up at your doorstep or at the table next to you. They will start saying things that surprise even them. They'll ask for something—they are not sure what—and wait for your reply."[5]

### Making It Personal

I am always amazed that whenever God answers the "send me" prayer, He has also made sure the person He is sending is uniquely qualified to fulfill the assignment. God has shaped you to serve through your experiences, education, gifts, personality, passions, and relationships. God has people and situations that you are divinely prepared to touch.

I wonder what God has in store for you *today*. I am curious as to what adventure He may want to send you on, if you are willing to go. Ask God to send you today, and be ready for an adventure that will make a difference in people's lives.

### NOTES

[1]Adapted from Dave Earley, *Prayer Odyssey* (Shippensburg, PA; Destiny Image, 2004), p. 14.

[2]Henry Blackaby and Claude King, *Experiencing God* (Nashville, TN: Broadman and Holman, 1994), pp. 44–45. Used by permission.

[3]Ibid., pp. 45–46.

[4]Bruce Wilkinson, *The Prayer of Jabez* (Sisters, OR: Multnomah Publishers, 2000), p. 42.

[5]Ibid., p. 36.

# 15

## SAVE US:
### The Prayer of the Disciples
MATTHEW 8:25

*Sandy and Joe were sailing in the Gulf of Mexico when they were caught in an unexpected storm. The wind blew them far out to open sea. When the storm subsided, they drifted helplessly for two days, baking in the hot sun. Their water supply dwindled away. They knew their lives were in danger.*

*The couple prayed to God for help, but no help came.*

*Then Sandy prayed one more time. "Oh, Lord, You are our only hope. Please save us."*

*As she finished, she looked up and saw in the distance what appeared to be a cross coming toward them. She thought she must be hallucinating and blinked to clear her vision but there was indeed a cross on the horizon. She awakened her husband, Joe. He also could make out a cross moving in their direction.*

*As the cross drew closer, they could see that it was actually the masthead of a large yacht—and it was definitely coming their way! The couple stood up, waving their arms to attract attention.*

*When they were safely on deck, Sandy said, "It's*

*incredible that you found us! We thought we'd never
be rescued!" But what the yacht owner explained next
convinced Joe and Sandy that their rescue was no coincidence. The yacht had been traveling on automatic pilot
for several hours, but inexplicably the boat ended up
traveling ten miles off its intended course.*[1]

"Save us." You can be sailing along through life, making
progress and enjoying the trip, when out of nowhere a storm
arises. In seconds you are overwhelmed. Huge waves pound and
then launch you mercilessly into the air. Water pours relentlessly
into your boat faster than you can bail it out. Howling winds
whip you around and drive you far off course. You lose your
bearings and your hope. The gaping jaws of doom start to shut
around you.

No one is immune to the storms of life. Even if you are
doing all the right things and headed in the right direction,
storms will find you. The question is not *if* you will face them,
but *how* you will respond.

One of the most effective prayers in the Bible came from
the disciples as they sailed across the Sea of Galilee. At the time,
the ministry of Jesus was in high gear. The disciples were sailing
away from the crowds to get a rest when a storm arose. Matthew recorded the event:

*Then he got into the boat and his disciples followed him.
Without warning, a furious storm came up on the lake,
so that the waves swept over the boat. But Jesus was sleeping. The disciples went and woke him, saying, "Lord,
save us! We're going to drown!"*

MATTHEW 8:23–25

When they realized that the storm was too big for them, they did not even try to deal with it on their own. It was already way beyond their ability to handle. So they went to Jesus.

## Lord, save us!

When they came to Jesus they were able to say it all in three words: "Lord, save us!" There was no time for flowery speeches. This was not the occasion for sounding impressive by offering profound thoughts or multi-syllable words. This prayer had to be like an arrow, lean and pointed, directed to the heart of the matter.

They did not tell Jesus all the details about the storm. In fact, they did not even mention the storm. He already knew.

They did not tell Jesus how to save them. It was beyond them. They did not need Him to help them with their bailing or with lowering the sails. They needed Him to do something and do it now!

They just asked Him to save them.

> He replied, *"You of little faith, why are you so afraid?"*
> *Then he got up and rebuked the winds and the waves,*
> *and it was completely calm. The men were amazed and*
> *asked, "What kind of man is this? Even the winds and*
> *the waves obey him!"*
>
> MATTHEW 8:26–27

## Making It Personal

There are several simple lessons we can take away from this story.

1. *Storms are inevitable.* Storms aren't reserved for the wicked. These disciples were not men who were out on a whiskey-soaked

gambling cruise. They were not out in the boat cheating on their wives. They had not just robbed a bank and were fleeing from the authorities. They were not pirates raiding hapless vessels. They were the disciples of Jesus Christ.

You will face storms. They may be storms of discipline or storms of development, but they will come. Even God's greatest people in the Bible faced storms. Adam and Eve had a rebellious son. Noah faced a global flood and later his own failure. Joseph was thrown into a pit, sold as a slave, and then unjustly cast into prison. Moses lost his temper and murdered a man. Later he had the responsibility of leading a horde of immature whiners. David was forced to run for his life when his father-in-law, the king, grew jealous of his success. Nehemiah had a strong enemy. After his conversion, Paul was repeatedly beaten, imprisoned, and persecuted.

2. *Sometimes following Jesus leads us into storms.* The men in the boat were not Jonahs out on the sea, trying vainly to sail away from God's plan for their lives. They were not even out on the water fishing for fun or profit. They were only in the boat because they had followed Jesus there. It was Jesus who got into the boat in the first place.

There is a mistaken notion that following Jesus leads to immediate prosperity and peace. Not necessarily. Certainly, the way of the cross leads to life eternal and the glories of heaven. There is a day coming when there will be no more sickness or sorrow. But in the meantime, we will experience some mean times.

3. *Storms are tests of faith.* Before calming the storm, Jesus made the point that the presence of fear was an indication of the absence of faith. Faith is the prime necessity for pleasing God (Hebrews 11:6). Faith overcomes the world (1 John 4:4). Faith is the fuel of righteous living (Habakkuk 2:4).

Sometimes when storms hit I wonder if God really loves me. My life is being tossed by several storms as I write these words. I am ashamed to confess that I have been overwhelmed by my grief and stupidly said, "God, I thought You loved me."

The thinking is that if God really loved me, He would protect me from storms. But that clearly is not the case. Jesus loved these disciples, yet they found themselves in the midst of a deadly storm. God the Father loves God the Son, yet Jesus, the Son of God, was in a boat that was about to be swallowed by angry waves.

4. *Jesus goes with us through the storms.* Jesus was right there in the boat. On another occasion when the disciples encountered a storm at sea, Jesus came to them walking on the water. If Jesus did not go with us through the storms, then we would have good reason to be afraid. But He goes.

5. *Jesus can handle the storms.* No storm is too big, no wind too fierce, no wave too high. Jesus can handle all of it. Jesus was so unafraid of this storm that He was sleeping through it. Yet, He had the power to calm the waves with just a word.

I don't know what storms you are facing. Maybe the loss of your job, a serious illness, or the death of a loved one is sending you reeling. One of your children is in trouble or was in an accident or is in jail. You could be in the throes of a divorce. Just as Jesus was there for the disciples, and for countless others, He will be there for you. The solution may not be quick or painless, but Jesus can work it all for good. You know He can. Trust Him.

6. *We need to ask.* The disciples did not wait until the boat was capsized and they were hopelessly adrift in the dangers of the deep. They went to Jesus and asked Him to save them before waiting too long. Asking in prayer was often advocated

by Jesus. Here are some of my favorite requests:

> Matthew 7:7: "Ask and it will be given to you."
>
> Matthew 7:11: "How much more will your Father in heaven give good gifts to those who ask him!"
>
> John 14:14: "You may *ask* me for anything in my name."
>
> John 15:7: "If you remain in me and my words remain in you, *ask* whatever you wish, and it will be given you."
>
> John 15:16: "Then the Father will give you whatever you *ask* in my name."
>
> John 16:24: "Until now you have not asked for anything in my name. *Ask* and you will receive, and your joy will be complete."
>
> James 1:5: "If any of you lacks wisdom, he should *ask* God, who gives generously to all without finding fault, and it will be given to him."
>
> James 4:2: "You do not have, because you do not *ask* God."

If you find yourself in a storm right now, don't be afraid to ask God to save you.

## NOTES

[1]Bob Russell and Rusty Russell, *When God Answers Prayer* (West Monroe, LA: Howard Publishing Company, 2003), pp. 98–100.

# 16

## HAVE MERCY ON US:
### The Prayer of the Blind Men
MATTHEW 9:27

It is such a short tale that most people overlook it. In fact, the whole scene is played out in a mere five verses and less than one hundred words. Yet for two men it was the biggest, grandest, greatest, most beautiful event in their lifetimes. We don't even know their names, but we do know that these men prayed one of the most effective prayers in the Bible. Here's their story:

> As Jesus went on from there, two blind men followed him, calling out, "Have mercy on us, Son of David!" When he had gone indoors, the blind men came to him, and he asked them, "Do you believe that I am able to do this?" "Yes, Lord," they replied.
>
> Then he touched their eyes and said, "According to your faith will it be done to you"; and their sight was restored. Jesus warned them sternly, "See that no one knows about this." But they went out and spread the news about him all over that region.
>
> MATTHEW 9:27–31

They had most likely been born blind. Most probably they

had never experienced the inexpressible joy of seeing a sunset or watching the leaves on a tree blow in the wind. Instead of witnessing a rainbow arching across humid sky, they had only seen blackness. Twenty-four hours a day, seven days a week, 365 days a year, nothing but darkness. They had no hope of ever being freed from their prison of endless night.

Beyond the physical frustration of being blind, they had to face monumental social pressure. In their world, blind men were not considered to be whole. They did not marry and had difficulty getting a job. They were excluded from the synagogue as "unclean," based on the faulty belief that their sin was the cause of their handicap. They were doomed to a life with only the tiniest of joys and slimmest of blessings.

Yet, they had heard about Jesus. The local buzz was that this itinerant, unlicensed rabbi could heal the sick. He had been healing all around the area. Maybe, just maybe, He could heal them.

So out of their desperation they hunted this healer. Stumbling along in pained pursuit, they followed Him. To follow Jesus was to track the miraculous. Lame children walked. Demon-possessed folks were freed. A dead girl was even raised to life. Surely He could heal them. They had no other hope and no other plan.

Finally, one day they heard that He was just down the street within earshot. Raw excitement, anticipation, fear, desperation, pain, and joy overcame them. Shouting into the dark, they began yelling, "Have mercy on us, Son of David!" Again and again they cried out. A lifetime of blindness, years of living life as social outcasts, and dozens of dashed dreams prodded them on. "Have mercy on us, Son of David!"

**Have mercy.**

Jesus heard them and paused. Eagerly, cautiously, yet irresistibly, they came to Him. Calmly He asked, "Do you believe that I am able to do this?"

We don't know if they paused and added up their faith or if they just blurted out their answer. All we know is that they said, "Yes, Lord."

All the time they had been on His trail, they had thought up long speeches as to why He must heal them. Yet, in the crisis of decision all they had been able to say was "Have mercy on us" and "Yes, Lord."

But those words were enough. "Then he touched their eyes and said, 'According to your faith will it be done to you'; and their sight was restored."

A little prayer yielded a great big answer. The Bible record is so subtle and matter of fact. All it says is that their sight was restored. These wonderful words are not in all capital letters. They are not in rainbow colors. There is not even an exclamation point.

But you had better believe that as far as these two men were concerned, fireworks were going off. Cannons were booming. Meteors were shooting through the sky. Bands were playing. Dancers were dancing. Banners were flying. And they couldn't take it all in. I can hear them now, "Oh my, look at that! I can't believe it is so beautiful! Look over here. Did you see this?"

Then Jesus did something that tells me He has a wonderful sense of humor. The Bible says, "Jesus warned them sternly, 'See that no one knows about this.'"

Right! He had to be kidding. These men had been blind. They were without sight. They had spent a near eternity visually impaired. And with a simple touch He had totally, radically, wonderfully changed their worlds. Jesus must have had a smile on His face when He said it because it would be a greater miracle for them to keep quiet than it was for Him to heal them.

And they couldn't. Their story ends with these words: "But they went out and spread the news about him all over that region."

"Have mercy." Just two little words, yet they are so wonderfully powerful. And they still work today. Roy Mansfield is the dynamic young pastor of the Manhattan Bible Church in New York City. On Sunday, January 25, 2003, he had six strokes in one day and, for all practical purposes, should have died. Below are a few of the e-mails he sent his congregation and prayer partners.

*February 2, 2003*
*My dear friends,*

*As many of you are aware, one week ago last Sunday I had 6 strokes, and the next day I almost died in the ICU of Columbia Presbyterian Hospital. By Monday I am told there were probably 10,000–20,000 of God's people interceding for me. I am a living, breathing, talking, typing and even sometimes walking miracle. Even the doctors and nurses acknowledged God's healing in my life, as they watched person after person come into my room and pray for me. If you had not heard of my condition I am sorry to shock you, but I'm sure that many of you had heard of my condition and had prayed for me. I thought I would share with you every day or two a bit of how God had answered your prayers on my behalf.*

*I have been on the supernatural, super-accelerated Jesus recovery plan. If you continue to pray for me and*

*I continue on this recovery plan, I am hoping to attend church on Sunday and greet our people in the English and Spanish ministry. By God's grace, I hope to preach a week from Sunday (March 2nd). Thank you for your continued prayers.*

*February 9, 2003*
*Dear friends,*

*Thank you for you continued prayers. Two weeks ago I was having 6 strokes in St. Joseph's emergency room. Today I went to church and lifted my hands in praise (which I should not be able to do) and greeted our Spanish and English congregations. Please keep praying for me.*

*Roy*

*February 10, 2003*
*My dear friends,*

*[Mansfield begins by describing what happened the day after his six strokes. Then he tells the following story.] I had lots of visitors, and I seemed to be steadily improving. A very close friend told me that morning that God had led her to pray that He would "pour on the water" before the fire fell to bring Him glory. She was referring to Elijah's encounter with the prophets of Baal. Elijah poured water on the sacrifice before God sent His fire to consume it. Through this God's glory was magnified even more. I didn't really understand the implications of what God had led her to pray at the time. In essence she was praying that God would make things worse before He made them better, so that His glory would be magnified even more.*

*It became obvious that God had led her to pray in this way because about 1:00 a.m. I began to feel my entire right side go numb. Immediately, a whole team of doctors rushed into the room and began working furiously on me. They began trying to run I.V.'s and lines into every imaginable (and even unimaginable) part of my body. Again I was paralyzed but could see and hear and (unfortunately) feel everything that happened. They tipped my bed for my head to hang down so everything would rush to my head. I remember thinking, "Hey, this is just like on TV." Everyone was rushing frantically around me except for one doctor. I remember the doctor in charge standing motionless in all the frenzied activity, staring at me for several seconds. He soon disappeared, and I later found he went to talk to Natalie. He told her that they were doing everything they could, but the stroke kept progressing. He told her that it was possible for them to attempt a very high-risk procedure that had not been tried before on any patient in I.E. He said if they tried the procedure there was a great risk that I could die. If they did not, it was probable that I would spend the rest of my life unable to move any part of my body but my eyes.*

*Let me say that Natalie is not by nature a decision maker. When she has to decide on skim milk or 2% she relies heavily on the multitude of counsel. She was surrounded by church members, but nobody was saying anything. That's understandable. Who wants to make the decision that kills the pastor? Can you imagine, "And this is elder so-and-so, who killed our last pastor." Finally, one of our elders, Charles Delph, asked the doctor what he would do if it were one of his loved ones. He said that he would opt for the procedure. By that time there were probably 10,000–15,000 people praying for me. I understand God had led Victoria, from our church, to pray specifically that the doctors would be willing to try something new. I believe God took all those prayers and converged them in that room at that one climactic moment, and Natalie told the doctor to begin the procedure that God would use to save my life.*

*By this time I had stopped breathing and they had put a tube down into my lungs and put me on a respirator. I think I had the world's record for most stuff stuck in my body. . . .*

*After two hours the doctors were able to stabilize me. The lead doctor came back a couple of hours later and began to run the neurological tests on me. After each test he said one word, "Unbelievable."*

*I'll continue the story of God's grace in a day or two. If there is someone you know prayed for me, please thank them and feel free to forward this to them so they are able to rejoice with us in God's gracious answer to their prayers.*

*Thank you for your continued prayers,*

*Roy*[1]

God had healing mercy on Roy Mansfield. Today he has resumed his high-energy, high-intensity ministry. He is a walking miracle and living testimony of the power of God.

## Making It Personal

When it comes to physical affliction and healing, there are

several truths we know:

- God is able to heal any and all afflictions, including the ultimate affliction, death.

- Sometimes He uses modern medicine. Other times He circumvents medicine and heals without it.

- There are times when we ask and God says "No" to our healing because He has a higher purpose to accomplish. Instead of giving us healing mercy, He provides us with enduring grace.

- There are also occasions when His answer is "Wait."

- One day all of God's children will experience complete and permanent healing in heaven.

- It doesn't hurt to ask for mercy. The blind men chased Jesus down and asked for healing mercy. Roy Mansfield had thousands praying for him.

I don't know the nature or extent of your physical affliction. But I do know that God can't answer your prayer if you don't pray. Go ahead and ask. Pray, "Have mercy on me." Give God a chance to answer. And when He does, give Him the glory.

## NOTES

[1]Used by permission of Roy Mansfield, pastor of Manhattan Bible Church, New York, New York.

# 17

# LORD, TEACH US TO PRAY:

## *The Prayer of the Disciples*

### LUKE 11:1

"I'm just too busy."

"Even though I'm trying to go faster, I keep getting further behind."

"I am going as hard as I can, but I am not sure where it's getting me."

"I want to care about all the needs around me, but I just don't have enough strength."

Ever feel like any of the above? Wish you knew what to do?

At another time and in another place, twelve tired men wrestled with many of those gnawing frustrations. They were trying desperately to keep up with Jesus as He rolled through the daily onslaught of highly needy people and deeply challenging situations. Overwhelming dilemmas and staggering burdens flew at Jesus at a dizzying pace. Yet, He seamlessly flowed through each encounter with astounding grace, poise, and power. What was His secret? Where did He get His stunning inner strength and wonderfully winsome wisdom?

After careful observation the answer became clear. This Man had an exceptional prayer life. S. D. Gordon has summarized the central role prayer held in the life of Jesus:

*How much prayer meant to Jesus! It was not only His* regular habit, *but His resort in* every emergency, *however slight or serious. When perplexed He* prayed. *When hard pressed by work He* prayed. *When hungry for fellowship He found it in* prayer. *He chose His associates and received His messages* upon His knees. *If tempted,* He prayed. *If criticized, He* prayed. *If fatigued in body or wearied in spirit, He had recourse to His one unfailing habit of* prayer. Prayer *brought Him* unmeasured power *at the beginning, and* kept *the flow unbroken and undiminished. There was no emergency, no difficulty, no necessity, no temptation that would not yield to prayer, as He practiced it. . . . He prayed so much and so often that it became to Him like breathing— involuntary.*[1]

The disciples, noting the authority by which Jesus spoke, the compassion He showed the hurting, and His miraculous power, observed that all of it flowed from His prayer life. So when they had an opportunity to ask Him anything they wanted, they made this request: "Lord, teach us to pray." Luke's Gospel records the incident.

*One day Jesus was praying in a certain place. When he finished, one of his disciples said to him, "Lord, teach us to pray, just as John taught his disciples."*

LUKE 11:1

Somewhat innocently and inadvertently, the disciples stumbled onto one of the most effective prayers written in the Bible, "Lord, teach us to pray." This prayer could be considered the foundation from which all other requests are formed.

The disciples' request is supremely significant for several reasons. First, it was answered. Second, the answer changed their lives. Third, we can pray the same request today.

Jesus did not deny, ignore, or delay to answer their request. His affirmative response was immediate. That is because "Teach us to pray" is a prayer God loves to answer for several reasons. First, God delights in our prayers. Too often we wrongly assume that God tolerates our prayers when, in reality, He revels in them. In fact, they are so precious to Him that He collects them as beautiful bowls of incense perfuming His throne (Revelation 5:8). Because our prayers end up in heaven, they are some of a tiny handful of things that are eternal in nature. (The others are God, the Word of God, and the souls of people.)

God also wants to teach us to pray because prayer is conversing with God, and He loves to spend time with us. As people get older they can gain great insight and wisdom. I remember being with my mentor, Elmer Towns, on his sixtieth birthday. I asked him what was important to him at that age. Without a moment's hesitation he said, "Relationships—I have learned that relationships are the most important part of life." God already knows this and greatly prizes our prayers as they build our relationship with Him and Him with us.

Moreover, God is willing to teach us to pray because He has an immense Father's heart that loves us and wants to meet our needs. Prayer touches His heart and, therefore, is the key to everything else. Everything we need is at the disposal of prayer. Pastor David Jeremiah has written, "I scoured the New Testament some time ago, looking for things God does in ministry that are not prompted by prayer. Do you know what I found? Nothing. I don't mean I had trouble finding an item or two:

I mean I found *nothing*. Everything God does in the work of ministry, He does through prayer. Consider:

Prayer is the way you defeat the devil (Luke 22:23; James 4:7).

Prayer is the way you get the lost saved (Luke 18:13).

Prayer is the way you acquire wisdom (James 1:5).

Prayer is the way a backslider gets restored (James 5:16–20).

Prayer is how saints get strengthened (Jude 20; Matthew 26:41).

Prayer is the way to get laborers out to the mission field (Matthew 9:38).

Prayer is how we cure the sick (James 5:13–15).

Prayer is how we accomplish the impossible (Mark 11:23–24).

. . .everything God wants to do in your life He has subjugated to one thing: Prayer."[2]

When the disciples prayed, "Lord, teach us to pray," Jesus answered by giving them what has become the most popular pattern for prayer ever uttered. Often called the Lord's Prayer, this sample prayer provides amazing and timeless insights into the hows and whys of prayer.

*He said to them, "When you pray, say: 'Father, hallowed be your name, your kingdom come. Give us each day our daily bread. Forgive us our sins, for we also forgive everyone who sins against us. And lead us not into temptation.' "*

LUKE 11:2–4

This is a wonderful, simple, eloquent, robust, rich little treasure of a prayer. Most scholars agree that this is not merely a prayer to be prayed verbatim by rote. This prayer serves as a road map for prayer, providing an outline of the key elements of prayer. This model prayer has six primary points:

Adoration: "Father, hallowed be your name."

Submission: "Your kingdom come."

Petition: "Give us each day our daily bread."

Confession: "Forgive us our sins."

Forgiveness: "Forgive everyone who sins against us."

Protection: "Lead us not into temptation."

Several years ago I made it my habit to take a prayer walk every morning using this prayer as my outline. The moment I walk out the door and down the driveway, I begin, "Our Father in heaven, hallowed be your name." At that point I launch into a season of adoration, such as "I praise and worship You today because there is none like You, You are creative and make all things beautiful in Your time, You are mighty beyond compare," and so on. Many great prayer warriors have used this prayer as their guide.

Note carefully the exact words of the disciples' request. They said, "Teach us *to* pray." They did not ask, "Teach us *how* to pray." They recognized that the key *to* praying is found *in* praying.

The deepest secrets and greatest experiences of prayer

cannot be revealed in books or lectures. Indeed, the most personal and powerful experiences are when we are on our knees, in our prayer closets, at the throne of God. Chester Toleson and Harold Koenig have written, "We don't really need to know a lot about prayer or prayer techniques. What we need to do is practice it. The more we pray the more we understand it and prosper from it."[3] Bible scholar Andrew Murray said, "Reading a book about prayer, listening to lectures, and talking about it is very good, but won't teach you to pray. You get nothing without exercise, without practice."[4]

Also note that the disciples did not say, "Teach us to preach, pastor, sing, serve, do miracles, or testify." They said, "Lord, teach us to *pray*." They recognized the great importance of prayer. As Oswald Chambers has reminded us, "Prayer does not fit us for the greater works; prayer is the greater work."[5]

And did the disciples pray! When Jesus ascended into heaven, they immediately convened a ten-day prayer meeting (Acts 1:14, 24). When the church was born, they transcribed prayer into its DNA (Acts 2:42). In the face of persecution they fell to their knees in prayer (Acts 4:24–31). As administrative responsibilities increased, they refused to be sucked into the tyranny of the urgent and instead reprioritized prayer as the most important task (Acts 6:4). Difficult decisions were made as the result of prayer (Acts 1:24, 6:6). When deadly opposition grew intense, prayer became more intense (Acts 12:5). If nothing else, and driving all else, the disciples were men of prayer.

## Making It Personal

"Lord, teach us to pray" is the foundation on which our prayer lives can be built. It acknowledges that God is the teacher and prayer is the course. Once we start praying, we can begin to experience the riches of prayer as well. And make no mistake, there are untold treasures awaiting you in the place of prayer. Success, blessing, direction, fulfilled dreams, forgiveness, wisdom, and miracles are available. The treasures of strength, deliverance, expanded ministry influence, help in raising children, mercy, healing, faith, and freedom from the prison of resentment have been discussed through the pages of this book and are experienced in the place of prayer.

Here are some additional "prayer helps."

1. *A time to pray.* Try to determine a set time each day when you will read a chapter of this book and pray. It could be first thing in the morning or the last thing at night or even over your lunch hour.

2. *An amount of time for prayer.* There are 24 hours in a day or 1440 minutes. Setting aside 15, or 20, or 30 minutes a day for study and prayer can become a life-changing experience.

3. *A place for prayer.* Jesus spoke of a prayer closet. Your place could be at a desk or the kitchen table or on your bed, or you could take a "prayer walk."

4. *A friend to pray with.* Jesus promised added insight and answers when two or more agree in prayer (Matthew 18:19). Ask a friend to read this book along with you. Gather together face to face, over the phone, or by e–mail, and pray together through the prayers you are learning.

One last piece of advice. . .don't wait any longer. Determine that you won't put off prayer one more day. In fact, why don't you begin by praying the disciples' prayer, "Lord, teach me to pray"? Spend some time in prayer asking God to help you do your part so you can grow as much as possible as a person of prayer.

# NOTES

[1]S. D. Gordon, *Quiet Talks On Prayer* (Grand Rapids, MI: Baker Book House, 1980), pp. 209, 233.

[2]David Jeremiah, *Prayer: The Great Adventure* (Sisters, OR: Multnomah Publishers, 1997), pp. 40–41.

[3]Chester Toleson and Harold Koenig, *The Healing Power of Prayer* (Grand Rapids, MI: Baker Book House, 2003), p. 66.

[4]Donald S. Whitney, quoting Andrew Murray, *Spiritual Disciplines for the Christian Life* (Colorado Springs, CO: NavPress, 1991), p. 66.

[5]Oswald Chambers, *Prayer—A Holy Occupation* (Grand Rapids, MI: Discovery House, 1992), p. 7.

# 18

# LORD, HELP ME:

*The Prayer of a Desperate Mother*

MATTHEW 15:25

No one on earth has the power to break your heart like your own child. Seeing them hurt and watching them struggle is a gut-wrenching, soul-shaking experience. You feel their pain. They have the power in a split second to bring tears to your eyes. When they make you proud, joy explodes in your heart that cannot be contained. When they disappoint you, it is like a knife jabbed deep into your heart. When they are treated unjustly, righteous indignation overwhelms your common sense. And when they hurt, you would do anything you could to take their place.

As I write this, I have three boys in high school. From the hospital, to the awards banquet, to the church platform, to the police station, to the prom, and yes, to the emergency room, Cathy and I have ridden the emotional roller coaster of parenting. I have cried, laughed, prayed, worried, lost sleep, and made more sacrifices as a parent than in any other role in life.

Among the many prayers I pray as a dad have been "Give me wisdom," "Give me success," and "Strengthen my hands." I have asked God to protect my children, bless them, grow them, and use them. But as parents sometimes the need is greater than our resources.

In Matthew 15, we find the very special prayer that is the cry of a desperate parent. As Jesus was resting from His heavy schedule in a non-Jewish region east of the Mediterranean Sea, He encountered a desperate mom.

> *A Canaanite woman from that vicinity came to him, crying out, "Lord, Son of David, have mercy on me! My daughter is suffering terribly from demon-possession."*
>
> MATTHEW 15:22

There is much we don't fully understand about demon possession. We do know that it has ugly, physical results and emotional expressions. We recognize that those possessed by the evil one are in extreme pain. We see that while human medicines may relieve symptoms, they are ineffective to produce lasting cures. We can appreciate the challenge that modern psychology faces in adequately understanding, explaining, or dealing with such a curse.

Most of all, we can confidently affirm that it was overwhelming to this mother to see her daughter experience such anguish of the soul. But when this mother cried out to Jesus for mercy, He did not answer.

> *Jesus did not answer a word.*
>
> MATTHEW 15:23

As a follower of Jesus, I find it most difficult to deal with the unexplained silences of God. You have been there. You have a legitimate need. You have come to the right source for help. You ask for mercy but all you get in response is the thundering silence of God. Most people would quit at this point.

This woman, a Canaanite, was used to the unresponsiveness of her gods. This was not new to her. She could have easily marked Jesus down as just as uncaring or impotent.

But she didn't.

*So his disciples came to him and urged him, "Send her away, for she keeps crying out after us."*

MATTHEW 15:23

Still, she badgered them for help. She kept coming for relief. Her pain was greater than her pride. After she persisted, Jesus answered.

*He answered, "I was sent only to the lost sheep of Israel."*

MATTHEW 15:24

Thanks a lot! He didn't even speak directly to her. He made this comment to His disciples. It was not what she wanted to hear.

She knew that she had no right to ask a Jewish man to help her. She knew that she had no basis for expecting Him to respond. But she had heard that He was mighty and compassionate. And she was desperate. So she pressed the issue ahead.

*The woman came and knelt before him. "Lord, help me!" she said.*

MATTHEW 15:25

**Lord, help me.**

What a simple prayer! "Lord help me." What a powerful prayer!

With all of her faith, all of her emotions, and all of her love for her daughter, she prayed. The weight of her need, every ounce of her hurt, and the totality of her helplessness were embodied in those three little words, "Lord, help me."

What do you say when you have nothing else to say? What words can better express the burden of the broken-hearted parent? "Lord, help me."

What is your pressure point of pain today? What about your child's situation is overwhelming you? What burden is completely beyond your control? Where do you need help?

"Lord, help me." Say the words slowly. See the suffering soul of your beloved child. See your own empty hands. See the all-sufficient Savior. Bow before Him and speak your heart.

Jesus was moved to act on her behalf.

> He replied, "It is not right to take the children's bread
> and toss it to their dogs."
> "Yes, Lord," she said, "but even the dogs eat the crumbs
> that fall from their masters' table." Then Jesus answered,
> "Woman, you have great faith! Your request is granted."
> And her daughter was healed from that very hour.
>
> MATTHEW 15:26–28

Read verse 28 again. First, Jesus commends her faith. Then He promises that her request is granted. Her little prayer had produced a big answer and her daughter was healed.

## Making It Personal

What can we learn from this desperate mom?

*Prayer needs all the faith we have.*

Jesus said, "Woman, you have great faith!" A look back through this passage gives us some insights into the type of faith

141

she displayed. As a Canaanite, non-Jew, and not yet a devoted follower of Jesus, she had great faith. Her faith was great for the little amount of truth and light she had been given. She had not had the privilege of growing up hearing about the powerful love of the God of the Bible. This was a new venture for her. She had to turn from pagan deities in order to trust in Jesus to help her. She was way out of her comfort zone. Coming to Jesus, persistently asking and not giving up until she was helped, took all of the faith she had.

1. *Prayer needs faith that refuses to quit.* We don't fully understand the ways of God. We do know that sometimes God holds off answers in order to allow our faith to blossom fully. This desperate mother did not give up, even when she initially got no answer. She did not quit asking until the disciples again asked Jesus to do something. She continued asking even after He said "No." Her love for her daughter and her confidence in Jesus' ability to heal would not let her give up.

2. *Prayer needs faith that is humbly dependent.* Her faith was great because it was not based on her sense of worth but on her conviction that Jesus must eventually respond to those in need. If a master would give crumbs to dogs, then Jesus must surely answer the prayer of a Canaanite.

3. *Prayer works.*

*Then Jesus answered, "Woman, you have great faith! Your request is granted." And her daughter was healed from that very hour.*

MATTHEW 15:28

Her prayer worked. God heard her heart, saw persistent faith, honored her humble dependence, and touched her daughter. I can only imagine the joy that exploded in her heart. I bet she danced all the way home. She probably had a huge smile on her face for years to come.

It is a wonderful thing when God answers the prayers of desperate parents. And all parents get desperate at one time or another. Among many painful concerns, we wonder if they are well physically, who they are involved with, what college they will choose, or will choose them, and what career they will pursue.

Desperation takes over when children begin to take the path of prodigal living. One of my good friends and a fantastic worship leader, Andy Bullard, is the son of a dear pastor and his wife. In college, Andy went through a period of prodigal living. This is his story of how his father's love and prayer helped him realize that living for God is the only way.

*I grew up in a pastor's home. My parents loved God with all their hearts and were great parents! During the last two years of high school and the first two years of college, I slowly fell into a bad lifestyle of ignoring the Holy Spirit's conviction in my heart. I chose to get heavily involved with alcohol and partying.*

*One lonely night when I was twenty years old, I had been drinking and hanging out at a party. Someone came in and told me my dad was outside. It was about 2 a.m. I immediately felt this huge lump in my throat, and I walked outside. Ashamed, I approached my father, who calmly looked at me and said, "Son, the Holy Spirit woke me up a little while ago and I felt Him telling me to go take a drive. He told me, 'Your son is in trouble and needs you.' That's how I found you here. Andy, I believe God has a plan and design for your life and wants to use you for His glory, but if you keep on living like this, you're going to miss out on all of it. I love you—I'll see you at home."*

*That same weekend I was on my face before God, weeping and repenting for the way I had been living. I felt so dirty inside and decided, from that moment on, I would acknowledge God's greatness. I would fear Him and let Him change my life. By God's glory, I have not lived that kind of lifestyle since then. I know that God used my father and my mother and their prayers, love, and loving rebuke to draw me back to the Lord! I am so thankful for honest, praying and loving parents!*[1]

I recently spoke at a missionary training conference and had a wonderful time of fellowship with these pioneer servants of God. A mom who had heard me speak in previous years stopped me after my second day of teaching. The year before, she had told me of the difficult transition her children were having upon returning to the States from the mission field.

Then she said, "The first time we heard you speak, we were convicted to fast and pray for our children one day a week. But we did not do it. They had a very frustrating year that year. The next year we made a commitment to fast and pray for them one day a week. My husband and I would pray together over lunch. It was not easy," she said, pausing, with tears welling up in her eyes, "but it sure made a difference."

God loves our kids because He is their Father. He wants to give us all the help He can in raising them.

As I write this, my three teenage sons are all in high school at the same time. None of them is a shrinking violet or wallflower. They all seem to be gifted at getting themselves in a variety of complex situations. Like all pastors' kids and second or third generation Christians, they struggle to find their own faith relationship with God. As very human young men, they are not immune to temptation, trials, or troubles. Parenting three teenagers, while often a great deal of fun, is also very challenging. Parenting "just ain't easy." Almost daily I pray the prayer of the desperate woman, "Lord help me."

If you are a parent, this chapter has probably resonated with you on several levels. Learn to pray the prayer of the desperate mother for her daughter, "Lord, help me." If you do not yet have children, begin now to pray for the children that you may have in your future. Ask God to help you. Or pray for your nieces and nephews. Ask God to help them and their parents.

If you are past the point of having children, that's all right. Pray for Cathy, me, and our three boys. We need all the prayer we can get.

## NOTES

[1]Used by permission of Andy Bullard.

# 19

# INCREASE OUR FAITH:

## The Prayer of the Disciples

### LUKE 17:5

I appreciate the disciples. Their bald humanness shines out again and again. They repeatedly ended up with egg on their face or a foot in their mouth. Fear, doubt, ignorance, confusion, arrogance, and thick-headedness—they unwittingly displayed all of these and more. Reading about them in the Gospels never ceases to give me hope. If these guys could make it as disciples, then I have a chance.

One day Jesus was telling them about the need to repeatedly forgive repentant sinners. The disciples came back with a sincere yet comical response. Read it for yourself.

> *[Jesus said,] "So watch yourselves. If your brother sins, rebuke him, and if he repents, forgive him. If he sins against you seven times in a day, and seven times comes back to you and says, 'I repent,' forgive him." The apostles said to the Lord, "Increase our faith!"*

> LUKE 17:3–5

Don't you just love it? Jesus told them to offer forgiveness seven times a day if necessary. The very thought of such "radical forgiveness" seemed so beyond them that all they could say was "Increase our faith."

Somewhat innocently and inadvertently, the disciples again stumbled onto one of the most effective prayers written in the Bible, "Increase our faith." They could not have prayed a better prayer.

The Bible persistently points to the priceless personality of faith. Faith is portrayed as the requirement for pleasing God (Hebrews 11:6). It is to be central in our lives (Romans 1:17; Galatians 3:11; Hebrews 10:38). It is the means of salvation unto eternal life (John 3:16; Acts 16:31). Faith is the activity that leads to a right standing before God (Galatians 2:16) and pure hearts with God (Acts 15:9). Faith helps us walk in the light (John 12:36, 46) and experience spiritual life (John 20:31). It is the victory that overcomes the world (1 John 5:4).

Jesus continually exemplified and addressed the ability of faith in God to accomplish amazing things. The disciples heard Him commend the centurion for his great faith and then heal his servant without even seeing him in person (Matthew 8:5–13). They saw Jesus heal a paralyzed man because of the faith of his friends (Matthew 9:2). They witnessed Him heal a woman who had the faith to reach out and touch the hem of His garment (Matthew 9:23), blind men who had the faith to ask Him for mercy (Matthew 9:29), and a demon-possessed girl because of the persistent faith of her mother (Matthew 15:28).

They heard Jesus say that faith has the power to move mountains and uproot mulberry trees (Luke 17:6; Matthew 17:18–21; Mark 11:22–24). He also said that all things are possible to the person with faith (Mark 9:23). Later, He told them that faith was a key to answered prayer (Mark 11:24). He demonstrated the potential of faith to heal disease, cast out demons, and release the miraculous (Matthew 8:2–3, 8, 13; 9:20–22; Mark 9:21–26).

The one thing Jesus repeatedly rebuked His disciples for and warned them about was being of little faith (Matthew 6:30; 8:26; 14:31; 16:8; 17:20; Luke 12:28). The disciples cowered in the boat as the storm raged because they lacked faith (Matthew 8:23–27). After successfully walking on the water, Peter sank when he lost his faith (Matthew 14:22–33). The disciples were incapable of grasping spiritual truth when they lacked faith (Matthew 16:5–12). Likewise, they failed to cast out a demon (Matthew 17:14–21).

It would seem that the major lesson Jesus wanted them to learn from His ministry was to trust God. And they finally got it. After repeated bouts of fear and failure, they realized what they needed was faith, and lots of it. So when Jesus again challenged their level of spirituality by calling them to radical forgiveness, the light bulb went on. The "aha" moment arrived at last and they offered a short, sweet, powerful prayer.

### Increase our faith.

An initial reading of the rest of the chapter might lead you to believe that Jesus ignored their request. Not so. The answer to their prayer is not found in the rest of the chapter or even Luke's Gospel. To see how Jesus answered, you need to look at the book of Acts, Luke's follow-up to his Gospel. It is a book that could well be titled "The Acts of the Holy Spirit through the Apostles."

The great faith of the disciples is on display in every page of the first half of the book of Acts. While the word *faith* is not always used, the concept is demonstrated through every event described.

In chapter one the disciples' faith had grown enough to pray down the outpouring of the Holy Spirit on the day of Pentecost, ushering in the birth of the church. In chapter two

Peter's fearless faith was front and center as the previous coward stood before thousands and boldly proclaimed the Resurrection of Jesus. His courageous faith led to the conversion of three thousand!

In chapter three the strong faith of Peter and John led to the miraculous healing of a lame man. Peter explained it this way:

> *By faith in the name of Jesus, this man whom you see and know was made strong. It is Jesus' name and the faith that comes through him that has given this complete healing to him, as you can all see.*

> ACTS 3:16

Later, faith spurred Peter to preach to another huge crowd about the crucifixion and resurrection of Jesus.

Chapter four shows Peter and John being arrested for their brave preaching. By faith they fearlessly proclaimed the resurrected Christ in the face of stern opposition and refused to be silenced. After their release, the other disciples joined them in a faith-saturated prayer for greater boldness in the face of greater persecution, not deliverance from it.

Chapter five is the dramatic account of Ananias and Sapphira being exposed by Peter for lying to the Holy Spirit and the consequences of such an act. It also shows the powerful faith of the apostles as they did many signs and wonders and were even thrown in jail for their Christian witness. Subsequently, they were released by an angel and walked away, only to be brought before the authorities again. Their daring faith led to a beating but also shook the Jewish leaders to the point of letting them go.

Chapter six opens with wisdom-producing faith as the

disciples develop a plan and select personnel to meet a logistical nightmare. They selected their ministry assistants on the basis of their faith (Acts 6:5). Chapters six and seven tell how one of their disciples, Stephen, a man "full of faith and power" (Acts 6:7), had been deeply challenged by the contagious faith of the apostles to preach Jesus so boldly that he was killed, becoming the first Christian martyr.

As the flames of fierce persecution swelled, the faith of the disciples became evident in the lives of *their* disciples. Chapter eight tells how they began to spread the gospel out from Jerusalem to Samaria and beyond. Both an influential sorcerer and an Ethiopian eunuch came to saving faith through their testimony.

In chapter ten the gospel jumped across racial and ethnic divides to reach the Gentiles. The instrument was Peter, the man whose faith had failed the night Jesus was arrested.

In chapter twelve the faith of the early church is severely tested. James, the brother of John, was arrested and executed. Herod, sensing a public relations bonanza, arrested Peter and put him under the guard of sixteen men who watched him four at a time, in four-hour shifts. During that time he was chained between two of the soldiers while the others guarded the door.

The church turned this problem into prayer and faced the battle on their knees. God heard and sent an angel, who suddenly appeared by Peter's side. Immediately the chains fell from his wrists. Unnoticed, Peter walked past the guards and the guard posts to freedom. Peter went looking for his friends and ended up being the surprise guest at his own prayer meeting!

The disciples prayed, "Increase our faith," and God did. These men, who had been guilty of being of little faith, ended up as men of outstanding faith. They had enough faith to launch the church less than two months after seeing Jesus brutally executed in Jerusalem. They had enough faith to continue preaching in the face of withering persecution. All would face torture and horrible deaths.

Church history is rich in describing the martyrdom of the church's founders. Church historian Gottlieb Schumacher researched the lives of the apostles. He discovered that Matthew suffered martyrdom in Ethiopia, killed by a sword wound. John faced martyrdom when he was boiled in a huge basin of boiling oil during a wave of persecution in Rome. Miraculously delivered from death, he was then sentenced to the mines on the prison island of Patmos.

Peter was crucified upside down on an X-shaped cross because he told his tormentors that he felt unworthy to die in the same way that Jesus Christ had. James the Just, the leader of the church in Jerusalem, was thrown a hundred feet down from the southeast pinnacle of the temple when he refused to deny his faith in Christ. When they discovered that he survived the fall, his enemies beat him to death with a fuller's club.

James the Greater, son of Zebedee, was ultimately beheaded at Jerusalem. The Roman officer who guarded James watched in amazement as James defended his faith at his trial. Later, the officer walked beside James to the place of execution. Overcome by conviction, he declared his new faith to the judge and knelt beside James to accept beheading as a Christian.

Bartholomew, also known as Nathaniel, was a missionary to Asia. He witnessed to our Lord in present-day Turkey. Bartholomew was martyred for his preaching in Armenia when he was flayed to death by a whip.

Andrew was crucified on an X-shaped cross in Patras, Greece. After being whipped severely by seven soldiers, they tied his body to the cross with cords to prolong his agony.

His followers reported that when he was led toward the cross, Andrew saluted it in these words: "I have long desired and expected this happy hour. The cross has been consecrated by the body of Christ hanging on it." He continued to preach to his tormentors for two days until he expired.

The apostle Thomas was stabbed with a spear in India during one of his missionary trips to establish the church in the subcontinent. Matthias, the apostle chosen to replace the traitor Judas Iscariot, was stoned and then beheaded.

James the Greater, a son of Zebedee, was ultimately beheaded at Jerusalem. The Roman officer who guarded James watched amazed as James defended his faith at his trial. Later, the officer walked beside James to the place of execution. Overcome by conviction, he declared his new faith to the judge and knelt beside James to accept beheading as a Christian.[1]

## Making It Personal

1. *Big requests may take a while to be fully answered.* After asking Jesus to increase their faith, the disciples were not immediately men rich in faith. There were afraid to stand for Christ. Peter denied Jesus, Thomas doubted, and, except for John, the others abandoned Him. Their faith did not blossom until after the resurrection.

Although God is able to give us big answers instantly, we may not be ready to handle them. After asking for increased faith, the disciples had to grow through character-building experiences. God is always believable and trustworthy, but we have to grow into the type of people who can fully trust Him.

2. *We are the key to the answer of some of our prayers.* Faith is a choice. God can provide the reasons to believe, but belief is ultimately our choice.

3. *God delights in faith and is willing to answer our request for more.* Of all the things we can ask for, faith is one that God is always ready to give. So why not ask?

## Notes

[1]Grant R. Jeffrey, *The Signature of God* (Toronto, Canada: Frontier Research Publications, Inc., 1996), pp. 254–57.
Note that the details of the martyrdoms of the disciples and apostles are found in traditional early church sources. These traditions were recounted in the writings of the church fathers and the first official church history written by the historian Eusebius in AD 325. Although we cannot at this time verify every detail historically, the universal belief of the early Christian writers was that each of the apostles faced martyrdom faithfully without denying their faith in the resurrection of Jesus Christ.

# 20

# GOD, HAVE MERCY ON ME, A SINNER:

## The Prayer of the Tax Collector

LUKE 18:13

How do you know if God is really listening to your prayer? How can you be sure that your request is the type of petition that He likes to answer? What sort of demeanor impresses God?

Jesus wanted to help us understand the answers to these questions. Being the world's best teacher, He told a tale of two men that answers these questions and more.

> *To some who were confident of their own righteousness and looked down on everybody else, Jesus told this parable: "Two men went up to the temple to pray, one a Pharisee and the other a tax collector. The Pharisee stood up and prayed about himself: 'God, I thank you that I am not like other men—robbers, evildoers, adulterers—or even like this tax collector. I fast twice a week and give a tenth of all I get.' But the tax collector stood at a distance. He would not even look up to heaven, but beat his breast and said, 'God, have mercy on me, a sinner.' I tell you that this man, rather than the other, went home justified before God. For*

*everyone who exalts himself will be humbled, and he who humbles himself will be exalted."*

LUKE 18:9–14

This short parable contains a diminutive prayer that produced a dynamic answer. But before we can fully appreciate the prayer, we need to understand the context.

1. *The Audience.* Jesus, in the presence of His disciples, was specifically addressing "some who were confident of their own righteousness and looked down on everybody else." These were probably the Pharisees, since one of the two characters in the story was a Pharisee. The Pharisees, a Jewish sect, were strict observers of the Mosaic law of the Old Testament. They loved the external, detailed aspects of the law and, when it was not specific enough, they added their own traditions—hundreds of them. Unfortunately, these overzealous rule-keepers valued the outward keeping of their rules above all else. As a group, because they had become exceedingly self-righteous, they looked down on anyone who was not in their sect.

2. *The Setting.* The two men Jesus told about in the little story had one similarity and many differences. Their similarity was that both "went up to the temple to pray." For a Jew living during the time of Jesus, the temple was the prime place of prayer. When Solomon dedicated the first temple, his prayer was that God's eyes would be open to the temple day and night. It was to be the place where God would hear prayers and forgive (see 2 Chronicles 6:20–21).

Jews still view the temple in Jerusalem as the supreme location for prayer. Today in modern Jerusalem you can see Jews gathered at the Western Wall of the remains of Solomon's temple. This sacred place is often called the Wailing Wall and was believed to be the back wall of the Holy of Holies on the temple mount. Three times a day, for thousands of years, Jewish prayers from around the world have been directed toward the Western Wall.

Jewish mystical tradition teaches that all prayers from around the world ascend to the Western Wall, and from there, to heaven. The Talmud says, "If someone is praying outside the Land of Israel, he should direct his heart in the direction of Israel. If the person is praying in Israel, he should direct his heart toward Jerusalem. Those in Jerusalem should direct their hearts to the Temple."[1]

3. *The Main Characters.* In Jesus' story, one man was a Pharisee and the other, a tax collector. Jesus, no doubt, used these two types of men because they represented the extremes of the culture. The Pharisees represented the superficially upright, externally moral, legalistic, self-righteous, ultra-right wing of Judaism. The tax collectors signified the bad boys.

Because Israel was under Roman occupation, the Jews were saddled with a heavy tax burden. Tax collectors were Jews who collected taxes from their Jewish brothers and sisters for the Romans. This made them traitors in the eyes of their people. To make matters worse, often they were found to be guilty of extortion as well as associating with prostitutes and other "dregs of society."

You have to love it!

4. *The Ineffective Prayer of the Pharisee.*

*"The Pharisee stood up and prayed about himself: 'God, I thank you that I am not like other men—robbers, evil-doers, adulterers—or even like this tax collector. I fast twice a week and give a tenth of all I get.' "*

Luke 18:11–12

Good storytellers follow the axiom, "Show but don't tell." Skillfully Jesus shows us five reasons why God refused to respond to the Pharisee's prayer.

(a) He prayed from a position of self-promotion. When he prayed, he "stood up." It was customary for men to stand when they prayed at the temple. But this Pharisee was standing with an attitude. An amplified study of the language reveals that he took his stand ostentatiously. The posture of the prayer may say much about the nature of the prayer and the one praying. Proud men stand in order to be noticed, especially when they pray. The Pharisee's prayer was pretentious and showy—and God was not impressed.

(b) The Pharisee was self-centered. He "prayed *about* himself" [italics mine]. The King James Version says that he "prayed with himself." The New American Standard Version states that he "prayed to himself." His prayer was self-absorbed. It was to himself, with himself, and about himself. Self-centered people focus their conversations and prayers on themselves. God's heart is all about selflessness.

(c) The Pharisee was self-righteous. He prayed, "God, I thank you that I am not like other men—robbers, evil-doers, adulterers—or even like this tax collector." He is telling God all the bad things he is too good to do. This Pharisee views himself as too righteous to rob, do evil, or commit adultery. He saw himself as above such lowly behavior. Self-righteous persons love to point out and criticize the shortcomings of others. God does not need our help in seeing others' shortcomings.

(d) The Pharisee was self-absorbed. He prayed, "I fast

twice a week and give a tenth of all I get." He not only told God what he wouldn't do, but also what he did do that set him apart from ordinary sinful men. This man fit the description of Jesus' hearers—those "who were confident of their own righteousness and looked down on every-body else" (verse 9). Self-absorbed men like to speak of the good they do. The awesome God is not awed by our deeds of righteousness.

Rabbi Simeon, the son of Jochai, exemplified this kind of pride:

> *If there were only thirty righteous persons in the world, I and my son would make two of them; but if there were but twenty, I and my son would be of the number; and if there were but* ten*, I and my son would be of the number; and if there were but* five*, I and my son would be of the five; and if there were but* two*, I and my son would be those two; and if there were but* one*, myself should be that* one.[2]*

(e) Prayer is often a wonderful revealer of the heart. The Pharisee had a proud, self-promoting, self-centered, self-righteous, self-absorbed heart. But the main cause of his inefficiency in prayer was his *self-sufficiency*. He did not feel the need to ask God for anything. He had it all together and under control. The biggest problem with legalistic religion is that it quickly digresses to the point where God is no longer needed. For the Pharisee, prayer had become little more than a chance to brag.

## 5. *The Effective Prayer of the Tax Collector*

*"But the tax collector stood at a distance. He would not
even look up to heaven, but beat his breast and said,
'God, have mercy on me, a sinner.' "*

LUKE 18:13

Jesus began with the word "but," signifying that in every
way the tax collector was a contrast to the Pharisee. As a result,
the tax collector's prayer was highly effective. There are several
reasons why his prayer succeeded.

First, the tax collector was without pretense. He stood at
a distance. He did not consider himself worthy of a front and
center place at the temple. Instead of standing where he could
be easily seen, he was entirely unassuming.

The tax collector was also humble. Instead of staring confidently into heaven, he prayed with a bowed head. Modest people
bow their heads in deference to those they consider above them.

Further, he did not judge or condemn. He did not tell God
how much better he was than someone else. Instead of picking
at the splinter in the eye of another, his vision was overwhelmed
with the beam in his own.

Rather than tout his own righteousness, he simply called
himself a sinner. The tax collector knew better than to try and
bluff God or deny the obvious. He knew what he was—a sinner. Unlike the Pharisee, he was dependent. He did not think
he had it all together or could handle it. He knew he was insuf-
ficient. He knew his need and who could meet it. So he asked
God to supply.

When someone approaches God with the humble, dependent, unpretentious attitude of the tax collector, his or her heart

is attuned to real needs and right directions. The tax collector's prayer was right on target. He not only asked *for* something, he asked for *the right thing.*

God wants to answer our prayers, but so often we ask for the wrong things. We pray about nonessentials and miss the real needs of our hearts. This tax collector nailed the request, just as Solomon did when he asked for wisdom, and the disciples when they wanted to be taught to pray. The tax collector asked God for mercy. He offered one of the most effective prayers found in the Bible.

### Have mercy on me, a sinner.

Our relationship with God is founded upon God's mercy. As Isaiah witnessed, God is absolutely holy, without sin in any way, shape, or form. His level of holiness is so intense that the seraphim literally burn in the brilliant flame of His holiness.

We are not holy in any way, shape, or form. We are sinners by nature and deed, attitude and act. The wages of sin is death, and we deserve severe punishment for our continued sin. The best our righteousness merits is total and eternal banishment from God's presence and from blessing of any type.

Yet, God is merciful. He can rightfully withhold our punishment because His mercy drove Jesus to the cross in our place. The Father can spare us because He refused to spare Jesus. Jesus took our penalty. He died in our place. We can be saved.

Living in this consumer-centered, commercial-filled world, we are constantly being told that we have a *right* for more and better. Such a message may make for an effective advertisement, but it spells poor theology. The tax collector knew what he deserved, and it was not more or better. It was eternal separation from God in outer darkness. So instead of telling God that He must give him the great riches that were his right, he asked God for mercy so he would not receive the judgment he truly did deserve.

The word used here for mercy is *hilaskomai*, which is actually the word for an atoning sacrifice. In the fullest sense, the tax collector is saying, "God, be merciful to me through Your atoning sacrifice for sins, because I am a sinner."

The tax collector understood what too many miss. He knew that he could not merit a relationship with God through his own righteousness or good works. Paul summarized this reality:

> *For it is by grace you have been saved, through faith—and this not from yourselves, it is the gift of God—not by works, so that no one can boast.*
>
> EPHESIANS 2:8–9

## Making It Personal

If you never have before, now is the time to say to God the words uttered by the tax collector, "God be merciful to *me*, a sinner" [italics mine]. If you mean it, this can be a soul-saving, life-changing prayer. It was for the tax collector and it has been for untold others. Praying this is our part in being justified or made right with God.

> *"I tell you that this man, rather than the other, went home justified before God."*
>
> LUKE 18:14

Learn to pray as the tax collector, not the Pharisee. Lose any trace of arrogance, pretense, self-righteousness, self-centeredness, and self-sufficiency as you approach life in general and prayer in particular. Live and pray with humility, honesty, and modesty.

Come dependently to God in prayer. Learn to tell Him what you really need.

> *"For everyone who exalts himself will be humbled, and he who humbles himself will be exalted."*
>
> LUKE 18:14

## NOTES

[1]b. Berachot 30a.

[2]Adam Clarke, *Adam Clarke's Commentary on the Bible* (Nashville, TN: Abingdon Press, 1977), p. 401.

# 21

# FATHER, FORGIVE THEM:

*The Prayer of Jesus*

LUKE 23:34

It may have been the most difficult request ever made. It certainly was one of the most powerful.

I know you have heard this story before, but let me ask you to read through these facts as though they were contained in the lead story of today's newspaper.

In the previous twenty-four hours, Jesus had been through an emotional hell. A close follower selfishly betrayed Him so that Jesus would be unjustly arrested. One of His best friends denied knowing Him on three separate occasions. His other friends and followers deserted Him.

Alone, Jesus faced the most powerful men in His nation who had been plotting His death. They paraded Jesus through a ludicrous series of illegal trials. The savage soldiers who held Him decided to have some wicked fun, so they mocked and spit upon Him. The man who was judging His case turned Him over to these ruthless soldiers in order to have Jesus nearly flogged to death. Sadistic and brutal, they placed a crown of thorns on His head and then spit on Him.

A judge then brought Jesus before a bloodthirsty mob and let them decide His fate. Spurred on by the religious leaders, the people mercilessly cried out for His public execution. Afterward, forced to carry a cross up a hill through the center of town, the already half-dead Jesus was unable to make it on His own. Another man had to help.

At a place known as Skull Hill, Jesus' hands and feet were spiked into the wood of the cross with long metal stakes. There He was hung before the murderous mob, on the center cross between two convicted criminals. There he was left to fight for air while pulling His weight up and down against the metal spikes. The pain must have been excruciating.

Below Him the circus of the absurd continued. Religious leaders sneered at Him, and a cruel crowd scoffed. The whole scene was so hideous, so horrible, and so heinous that God the Father had to turn His back on His beloved Son. A dark cloud swallowed the hilltop as the afternoon sun refused to shine.

Yet, in the midst of the betrayal, denial, and desertion; despite the brutality, lies, and injustice; and in the middle of the murderous mayhem; Jesus said three of the most powerful words ever spoken.

### Father, forgive them.

How He did it, I cannot guess. It would have been totally unexpected and unnatural from anyone else. But Jesus, the victim in this awful passion play, was ever the victor.

"Father, forgive them." Three simple words powerfully summed up the reason for His life on earth. The bridge from God to man was paved with His blood and built on the foundation of forgiveness. His birth in Bethlehem, childhood in Nazareth, baptism in the Jordan, His miracles and teachings, and the Last Supper with His disciples were all scenes leading up to this moment. They all built steadily and relentlessly to this climax.

"Father, forgive them."

Jesus' prayer was powerfully answered. Dozens of those gathered around Jesus when He said those words found forgiveness. One of the thieves crucified with Jesus was pardoned with the promise of a home in paradise with Him. The Roman centurion who had overseen the crucifixion found forgiveness as he confessed Jesus to be the Son of God. Peter was forgiven for his denial, as were the other disciples for their desertion. Later, the debt of guilt owed by the priests in pursuing, or for some at least condoning, Jesus' death was cancelled for those who believed. Many members of that cutthroat crowd who cried for His crucifixion no doubt found forgiveness on the day of Pentecost or soon after.

Beyond the people who were in Jerusalem during Jesus' prayer, many others were to be forgiven as well. Three thousand from around the world found forgiveness on the day of Pentecost. Later, the message of forgiveness was taken to cities all over the known world of the first century.

Jesus' prayer of forgiveness has continued to echo throughout the centuries, as those of every tribe, tongue, and nation have experienced the cleansing joy of having their sins washed white as snow and cast into the depths of the deepest sea. God has been answering Jesus' prayer ever since it was uttered two thousand years ago.

I have been a recipient of the forgiveness Jesus prayed for on the cross. You see, my sins were part of what nailed Him to the cross. When He said, "Father, forgive them," He included *me.* And He included *you,* too.

When Jesus prayed, "Father, forgive them," He set us free from the prison of our sin. When we pray, "Father, forgive them," we set ourselves free from the prison of bitterness. Jesus described this prison in a story He told, which goes something like this.

Once upon a time long ago and far away, a man owed a king a massive, multibillion-dollar debt. But the king mercifully forgave him the entire amount.

Instead of celebrating his wonderfully good fortune, the forgiven man immediately went after a poor guy who owed him only a few thousand dollars. The poor guy couldn't pay, so the forgiven man had him locked up in debtors' prison. When the king heard what had happened, he was so upset that he restored the previously forgiven man's debt and threw him into the dungeon to be tortured.

This story reminds us that God has forgiven us a gigantic debt caused by our sin. Such forgiveness should prompt us to forgive others of the much smaller debts we feel owed to us because of offenses they may have caused. And it tells us that failing to forgive hurts us more than the other person. It locks us into a dungeon of torture and a prison of bitterness.

Although this prison does not have visible bars, chains, and torture chambers, they are every bit as real. When I am harboring bitterness in my heart toward another, I have unwittingly become a prisoner to them. Just the mention of their name can flood my mind with powerful and ugly thoughts. Seeing them elevates my heart rate and blood pressure. Hearing their voice can make me wince and cringe. Even when they are not around, I cannot get them out my mind. I am their prisoner and my bitterness toward them tortures me.

There is only one way out of the horrible prison of harbored hurts. There is only one key that turns the lock of freedom from the jail cell of resentment. It is the prayer Jesus prayed two thousand years ago, "Father, forgive them."

Praying this prayer is not optional for a healthy Christian—it is mandatory. As long as we live on earth, we will be hurt and offended by other people. We must learn to liberate them and set ourselves free in the process.

Lack of forgiveness is devastatingly powerful. It produces the awful fruit of resentment, bitterness, anger, hatred, strife, and jealousy. When we have unresolved hurts, we will find ourselves responding with insults, attacks, broken relationships, betrayal, and distance from God. Lack of forgiveness rips apart families, divides marriages, splits churches, and poisons friendships.

Recent studies have found wonderful physical healing and power in learning to forgive and great danger in not doing so. "Carrying around a load of bitterness and anger at how unfairly you were treated is very toxic," says Fred Luskin, Ph.D., director of Stanford University's Forgiveness Project. His researchers found that letting go of a grudge can slash one's stress level up to 50 percent. Volunteers in the study showed improvements in energy, mood, sleep quality, and overall physical vitality. Another study has shown that giving up grudges can reduce chronic back pain. And yet another experiment found practicing forgiveness limited relapses among women battling substance abuse.[1]

Physically, anger and resentment produce a steady stream of stress hormones, which then turn into toxins. According to Bruce McEwen, Ph.D., director of the neurological lab at Rockefeller University in New York City, these wear down the brain, leading to cell atrophy and memory loss. Stress also raises blood sugar, hardens arteries, and leads to heart disease. Yet, forgiveness stops these hormones from flowing. In a separate study of thirty-six men who had coronary heart disease and a history of painful hurts, half were given forgiveness training and half were not. The ones who forgave showed greater blood flow to their hearts.[2]

Forgiveness is not only beneficial for our physical and emotional well being, it is tremendously powerful spiritually. John Bevere recounts the story of a burly middle-aged man standing before a church in Naples, Florida, telling his story.

*"All my life I have felt like there was a wall between me and God. I would attend meetings where others sensed God's presence and I watch detached and numb. Even when I prayed there was no release or presence."*

*The man went on to tell how he realized that his problem was a lack of forgiveness. He continued, "I hated my mother for abandoning me when I was six months old. I realized that I had to go to her and forgive her. I called and spoke with her for only the second time in thirty-six years. I cried, 'Mom, I have held unforgiveness toward you all my life for giving me away.' She began to weep and said, 'Son, I hated myself for the last thirty-six years for leaving you.'" He continued, "I forgave her, and she forgave herself; now we are reconciled. Now the wall that separated me from God's presence is gone!"*

*Then the man began to weep so strongly he could barely get the next sentence out. "Now I cry in the presence of God like a baby."* [3]

## Making It Personal
Odds are good that there is someone who has inadvertently taken you prisoner because you have not forgiven their offense. Life is too short to be shackled with the ball and chain of an unforgiving heart. Our response to an offense determines our future. There are too many wonderful opportunities awaiting us when we take the way of escape from the dungeon of resentment.

Picture those who need your forgiveness and their offenses clearly in your mind. Make the choice Jesus made. Choose to forgive by praying one of the most powerful prayers in the world, "Father, forgive them."

## NOTES

[1] Lisa Collier Cool, "The Power of Forgiving," *Reader's Digest*, May 2004, p. 54.

[2] Ibid., p. 54.

[3] Adapted from *The Bait of Satan* by John Bevere, p. ix. Used by permission of Charisma House. Copyright 2004 by Strang Communications Co., USA. All rights reserved.

# 22

## FINAL THOUGHTS

After having read the twenty-one most effective personal prayers in the Bible, prayers that worked because God answered them positively, we should spend some time considering what we should do if God does not answer the way we had hoped. Or, what do we do when He does not seem to answer at all?

One reason God may be silent is sin. Sin can keep God from responding to our prayers.

*If I had cherished sin in my heart, the Lord would not have listened; but God has surely listened and heard my voice in prayer.*

PSALM 66:18–19

Sometimes God is silent because the request is too selfish.

*What causes fights and quarrels among you? Don't they come from your desires that battle within you? You want something but don't get it. You kill and covet, but you cannot have what you want. You quarrel and fight. You do not have, because you do not ask God. When you ask, you do not receive, because you ask with wrong motives, that you may spend what you get on your pleasures.*

JAMES 4:1–3

And at other times, God may not be responding because He is giving another message. He is saying, "Wait." Russell Kelfer's story illustrates this well.

Because Russell had always loved the written word, he decided to pursue a journalism degree at the University of Texas. However, after sustaining a sports injury to his eye, he was unable to complete the required reading. So he gave up his dream and joined the family business, Kelfer Tire Company. He took his place as the third generation of Kelfers to run the business.

Nearly twenty years later, Russell found himself teaching a home Bible study to single adults. As the group grew in number from 20 to 150, a local church asked him to teach the same material on Sunday mornings. What was to be a six-week Sunday commitment lasted the rest of his life. From those first classes, he developed a series of lessons, stories, poems, and audio and video tapes that would comprise his counseling and mentoring ministry. Today, Russell Kelfer's Discipleship Tape Ministry helps people around the world.

The boy who couldn't finish college because it required too much reading became the man God enabled to read, study, and write prolifically. Although Russell possessed no formal credentials for teaching, writing, or ministering, God gently led him into a ministry that used all of those skills. Russell often said, "I didn't have sense enough to be frightened."

From experience, he learned that God often answers our most passionate prayers with the frustrating response of "Wait." Russell's best-loved poem has ministered to thousands for the past twenty years because it speaks to our human desire to hear God's plan for our lives and our subsequent frustration when we feel we are met with His silence. What we often hear as God's "No," however, is often God's "Wait." God wants us to wait to "grow" our character, develop our faith, and thus fulfill His larger scheme.

## Wait
### by Russell Kelfer

*Desperately, helplessly, longingly, I cried;*
*Quietly, patiently, lovingly, God replied.*
*I pled and I wept for a clue to my fate. . .*
*And the Master so gently said, "Wait."*

*"Wait? you say wait?" my indignant reply.*
*"Lord, I need answers, I need to know why!*
*Is your hand shortened? Or have you not heard?*
*By faith I have asked, and I'm claiming your Word.*

*"My future and all to which I relate*
*Hangs in the balance, and you tell me to wait?*
*I'm needing a 'yes', a go-ahead sign,*
*Or even a 'no' to which I can resign.*

*"You promised, dear Lord, that if we believe,*
*We need but to ask, and we shall receive.*
*And Lord I've been asking, and this is my cry:*
*I'm weary of asking! I need a reply."*

*Then quietly, softly, I learned of my fate,*
*As my Master replied again, "Wait."*
*So I slumped in my chair, defeated and taut,*
*And grumbled to God, "So, I'm waiting for what?"*

*He seemed then to kneel, and His eyes met with mine. . .*
*and He tenderly said, "I could give you a sign.*
*I could shake the heavens and darken the sun.*
*I could raise the dead and cause mountains to run.*

*"I could give all you seek and pleased you would be.*
*You'd have what you want, but you wouldn't know Me.*
*You'd not know the depth of my love for each saint.*
*You'd not know the power that I give to the faint.*

*"You'd not learn to see through clouds of despair;*
*You'd not learn to trust just by knowing I'm there.*
*You'd not know the joy of resting in Me*
*When darkness and silence are all you can see.*

*"You'd never experience the fullness of love*
*When the peace of My spirit descends like a dove.*
*You would know that I give, and I save, for a start,*
*But you'd not know the depth of the beat of My heart.*

*"The glow of my comfort late into the night,*
*The faith that I give when you walk without sight.*
*The depth that's beyond getting just what you ask*
*From an infinite God who makes what you have last.*

*"You'd never know, should your pain quickly flee,*
*What it means that My grace is sufficient for thee.*
*Yes, your dearest dreams overnight would come true,*
*But, oh, the loss, if you missed what I'm doing in you.*

*"So, be silent, my child, and in time you will see*
*That the greatest of gifts is to truly know me.*
*And though oft My answers seem terribly late,*
*My most precious answer of all is still. . .Wait."*[1]

When the silence from God is not the result of sin and not a call to wait, it may be God's way of giving us a better answer. Prayers that appear to be unanswered may in reality be answered very well. If we think we are not getting results from our prayers, we should look again.

Too often we pray with the idea of "*my* will be done." We need to remember that we are part of the larger fabric of life. There are times when, instead of praying for relief from an affliction, it may be more important to pray for strength to accept and overcome the trouble. Then we will have grown in courage and patience and wisdom. The following poem by Francis of Assisi captures this insight.

*I asked God for strength, that I might achieve;*
*I was given health, that I might learn to obey.*
*I asked for riches, that I might be happy;*
*I was given poverty, that I might be wise.*
*I asked for power, that I might have the praise of men;*
*I was given weakness, that I might feel the need of God.*
*I asked for all things, that I might enjoy life;*
*I was given life, that I might enjoy all things.*
*I received nothing that I had asked for—*
*Everything I had hoped for.*
*My prayers were answered.*

Remember, prayer is not dictation. Prayer is not telling

God what to do and His immediately doing it. Prayer is cooperating with God so that He can accomplish His will. Don't be discouraged when God says "Wait," or when He gives you something other than what you asked. Remember, Father always knows best.

## NOTES

[1]Poem copyright 1977 by Russell Kelfer. Used by permission of Martha L. Kelfer, president, Discipleship Tape Ministries, Inc. For more information, visit www.dtm.org.

# ALSO FROM
# BARBOUR PUBLISHING

## NEVER GIVE UP
by Scott Dickson
The former CEO of Vanguard Airlines offers seven
life principles for navigating tough times.
ISBN 1-59310-144-9
192 pages

## MOMMY'S LOCKED IN THE BATHROOM
by Cynthia Sumner
A mother of young children provides tips and inspira-
tion for handling the physical and emotional stresses of
motherhood.
ISBN 1-58660-979-3
192 pages

## HOW TO RETIRE WITHOUT RETREATING
by Johnnie Godwin
An active retiree shares insights on the mental and
spiritual preparations for "life's best chapter."
ISBN 1-59310-447-2
256 pages